D1258275

The People of Georgia

AN ILLUSTRATED HISTORY

Mills Lane

A Beehive Press Book

LIBRARY OF GEORGIA

Savannah · 1992

"Delta College Library

JAN 1993

F
286
.L36
1992

FRONTISPIECE
Rural family, Greene County, May, 1939
Marion Post Wolcott, Library of Congress

Second edition © 1992 by The Beehive Press
© 1975 by The Beehive Press (first edition)

This book was edited by The Beehive Press,
which retains all rights to its contents and design.
This book is published by The Beehive Foundation
without profit or compensation to The Beehive Press.
The Beehive Foundation gives copies of its books
to college and public libraries throughout Georgia
and also sells them to individuals by mail.

Library of Georgia
℅ The Beehive Foundation
321 Barnard Street
Savannah, Georgia 31401

CONTENTS

Introduction:
Southerners and Americans

UNTIL the last few years, American history seemed to be a celebration of national innocence and virtue, generosity and power. This was our inheritance from the ideals of the Revolution, Jeffersonian and Jacksonian Democracy, the Civil War, the Progressives and the New Deal. This was what we called our economic destiny—immigrants coming to the new continent, sweeping through virgin forests, creating a new society free of the constraints of the Old World. Our confidence in this materialistic progress suffused our foreign policy, and clad it with virtuous trappings, from the Open Door in China, to two world wars and the Cold War. But Southerners seemed excluded from this view of American history, for it was hard to reconcile the sad fatalities of our unhappy regional past—the moral guilt of slavery and segregation, the frustrations of military defeat followed by military occupation, the region's social and economic backwardness—with the inherited belief in the American Dream. Like individuals who must find identities for themselves, accepting weaknesses and discovering strengths, before they can face constructively the world around them, so Southerners must come to terms with their past. In the 1990's, when all Americans are facing a crisis of national nerve, an honest look at our history may help reaffirm the essentially hopeful and unifying lessons of the American experience.

From its outset Georgia was the last and poorest colony at the southern extremity of the British empire in America, a rude and crude

7

W. H. Holmes plowing sweet potatoes,
Greene County, November, 1941.
Jack Delano, Library of Congress

place caught in a triangular struggle between France, Spain and England to control that part of North America after 1700, and a near disaster as an imperial enterprise. Georgia's reputation as a haven for weak and impotent persons was established from the outset, though perhaps only a handful of debtors ever came to Georgia, and the colony soon attracted a cosmopolitan assortment of international fugitives. In 1740 Henry Garrett wrote from the struggling military outpost which was then colonial Georgia: "I got into a very bad corner of the world, where poverty and oppression abound to such a degree that it's become proverbial this way to say 'as poor as a Georgian.'" After the Revolution, Georgia remained one of the last seaboard states to establish a stable society, for the removal of the Indians was a slow, difficult experience, not completed until 1838. La Rochefoucauld, an exiled peer of France who came to Georgia in 1796, called frontier Georgians the most barbarous, drunken, disorderly and reckless people in America. After the invention of the cotton gin in 1793, the South's preoccupation with cotton and slaves delayed the creation of a middle-class society of shopkeepers, workers, factories and cities. From his train, as it moved toward Macon during the Civil War, William Howard Russell viewed the social landscape of an enduring frontier: "From the windows of the carriages we could see that the children were barefooted, shoeless, stockingless — that the people who congregate at the wooden huts and grogshops of the stations are rude, unkempt, that the villages are miserable places." The Civil War disrupted Southern life, destroyed property and wealth and brought a social revolution which was not accepted for a century. For the next three generations, Georgians continued to live close to the land, farming, fishing and mining for their livelihood, retreating further toward regional isolation and suffering terribly as their agricultural system collapsed.

By the American standards that "bigger is better," that "nothing

Mrs. Ira C. Brown with her canned goods, Union Point, November, 1941.
Jack Delano, Library of Congress

succeeds like success," that "change is progress," this Southern history has been a failure. The Puritan ethic, popularized by outspoken American figures from Cotton Mather in the eighteenth century to Horatio Alger in the nineteenth, taught that hard work and virtue were rewarded with success, a doctrine which excluded most Georgians from grace. During the angry controversies leading to the Civil War, Georgians were described as ignorant, rude, bigoted, uncultivated and cruel people who delighted in oppressing their slaves and who had been made lazy and corrupt by a sinful institution. In the aftermath of the Civil War, the victorious side found every evidence of the moral decay, lack of free institutions and Northern enterprise which had foredoomed the Southern cause in its view. In 1865 Sidney Andrews surveyed Newnan, Georgia, where he recognized everywhere the symptoms of Southern inferiority: "Newnan is just like every other Southern town—streets full of mud, holes and wallowing swine, fences in every stage of tumble-down ruin, sidewalks in every condition of break-neck disorder, yards full of sticks and stones and bits of every conceivable rubbish—everywhere a grand carnival of sloth and unthrift and untidiness and slovenliness—everywhere that apathy of shiftlessness so pitiful to the soul of a New Englander!" Carl Schurz wrote from Mississippi after travelling through Georgia in 1865: "I found all of my preconceived opinions verified most full, no, more than that. This is the most shiftless, most demoralized people I have ever seen." In 1908 the *New Republic* called Georgia "a country like Haiti, which must be supervised by a more civilized and enlightened society." In 1920 H. L. Mencken called the South "an awe-inspiring blank . . . of fat farms, shoddy cities and paralyzed cerebrums" and wrote of Georgia in particular: "A self-respecting European, going there to live, would not only find intellectual stimulation utterly lacking; he would actually feel a certain insecurity, as if the scenes were the Balkans or the

Man selling bait, Augusta, August, 1936.
Margaret Bourke-White from You Have Seen Their Faces
(New York, 1937), with permission

China Coast. There is a state with more than half the area of Italy and more population than either Denmark or Norway, and yet in thirty years it has not produced a single idea." Though in 1931 Mencken awarded Mississippi the lamentable preeminence as The Worst American State, he ranked Georgia, out of the then forty-eight states, 45th in wealth, 46th in education, 43rd in public health, 46th in public order. Donald Davidson of Nashville parodied the legend of Southern barbarism portrayed by such sophisticates: "So the tale runs—a region full of little else but lynchings, shootings, chain-gangs, poor whites, Ku Kluxers, hookworm, pellagra, and a few decayed patricians whose chief intent is to deprive the uncontaminated, spiritual-singing Negro of his life and liberty. Over such pictures the East stormed, or shed crocodile tears, in the clever nineteen-twenties." Such criticisms were based partly on Southern problems—and partly on a denial of problems throughout American history and life.

But no longer can Americans from any region afford the luxury of self-satisfied self-righteousness. The American dream of unlimited opportunity and achievement will always be a real ideal and worthy of our pursuit, but it may have been the reality of American life only during the early nineteenth century. Our recent national history has demonstrated that the United States is not the perfect, powerful, innocent nation we had believed. The moral and military failure of the Vietnam War showed how essentially honorable, well-intentioned people could make honorable, well-intentioned mistakes. This was an important lesson for a nation committed to the idea that nothing succeeds like success and that good people win and bad people fail. Scandals in the administrations of presidents Nixon and Reagan—Watergate and Iran Contra—revealed moral failure in high and formerly respectable places. Once the South was obliged to accept black civil rights in the 1960's and 1970's, the greatest racial tensions and injustices, punctuated by explosive violence, remained in cities like Boston, New York, Detroit and Los Angeles. A binge of speculation and spending

Cotton chopper, White Plains, May, 1941.
Jack Delano, Library of Congress

in the 1980's, accompanied by scandals on Wall Street and deficit budgets in Washington, left us poorer and maybe wiser. As our national economic destiny passes to other emerging nations, the environmentalists continue to remind us that bigger is not always better. Riots in Los Angeles in the spring of 1992, followed by unrest in other cities, reminded all Americans of urban decay and problems of racism throughout all America. This crisis of national nerve frees Georgians and Southerners from the burden of an unrealized American dream. Now, at last, we can reexamine our regional past without romanticism or apology.

Beneath the layers of scholarly varnish, the essential history of Georgia is the story of good, simple people, black and white, living close together and close to the land, sharing great hardships and disappointments. Their history is the failure of an agrarian ideal, which James Oglethorpe, Georgia's founder, called "the Agrarian Equality," by which he meant a hope that a society of sturdy, independent yeoman farmers could live there in honest simplicity and self-respecting equality. But this hope was frustrated throughout Georgia's history — by the military preoccupations of the early colony which caused such great distress that most of the colonists fled from the place within the first ten years, by the expansion of slavery and plantations across the frontier which destroyed the foundations of a class of small farmers, by the Civil War debacle, by the development of sharecropping and farm tenancy at the end of the nineteenth century, and by the neglect of rural society in an urban, industrialized era. A tour of the Georgia countryside today, away from gleaming Atlanta and the white concrete ribbons of Federal highways, shows everywhere the abandoned farms, naked land, decayed buildings and languishing towns, which are the ruins of an agrarian world that has died. It is a melancholy scene which W.E.B. DuBois of Atlanta University described in 1901: "A feeling of silent depression falls on one as he gazes on this scarred and stricken land, with its silent mansions, deserted cabins and fallen fences." In this sense, Atlanta, populated in part by displaced rural people who

E. A. Marcus's son, Greene County, June, 1941.
Jack Delano, Library of Congress

could no longer live on the land and supported now by interstate commerce which has little to do with the economic life within Georgia, represents the failure and not the progress of Georgia since the Civil War.

Now, when the nationalizing, homogenizing pressures of our industrialized, urban society are bringing a real conclusion to state and regional history, Southerners had better pause to sift out and preserve the valuable traditions of their experience before they become too "American." Georgia was one of the greatest social and philanthropic experiments during the era of its establishment. The subsequent warts and pimples of Georgia history make us damned interesting. Southerners who now live in busy cities can find needed stability and humane values in the continuity and rhythm of their agrarian history. Southerners who now live in a consumption-oriented, cosmetic world of gratification and salesmanship can find a strong antidote in a plain and bittersweet account of their history. Indeed, Georgia's honest if humble history is important for all Americans, not just for Southerners. Thomas Wolfe wrote to his mother in 1923 that Southern promoters who shouted "Progress, Progress!" only meant more Fords, more Rotary Clubs, more Baptist Ladies Social Unions. After generations of Pollyanna platitudes about national triumph and righteousness, we Americans have become a reckless, selfish people, and we need some tenderness, tolerance, humility and humanity. Americans who have looked at their history superficially as a brittle story of success and reward may learn valuable lessons from the sad experience of Georgians who have already had to accept failure and disappointment. Now every American is called upon to reconcile himself to the reality of the nation's diminished role in world affairs and even her incapacity to solve her own national problems. The South's apparent "backwardness" may be only one obvious example of deep national imper-

Farm boy, August, 1936.
Margaret Bourke-White, Syracuse University Library

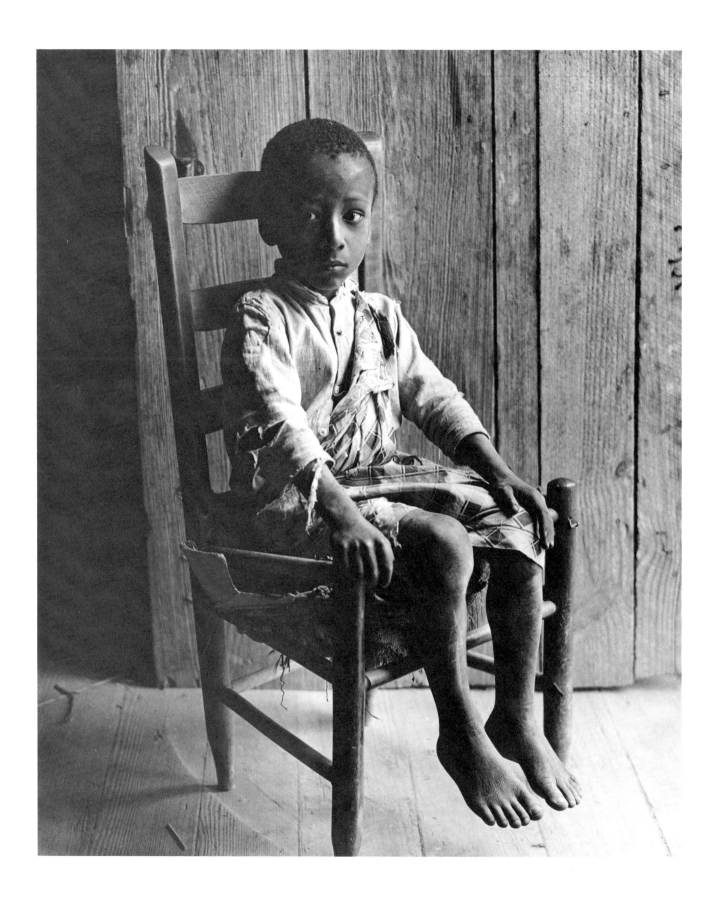

fection; certainly it is a common link to the poor and distressed condition of most people in our troubled world. Americans should understand that good exists beside evil, that poverty does not exclude happiness and that people can fail but still be admirable. In art, the ideal of beauty is based on an acknowledgement of imperfection. The real nobility of human experience is found not in triumph and riches but in struggle, courage, disappointment, perseverance against overwhelming odds and even in failure, itself. This is the great lesson of Georgia history.

This book was written nearly twenty years ago, and now the author, middle-aged and with a bald spot expanding as fast as his belly, returns to it. Though occasionally marred by the overwrought idealism of a young author, the lessons of *The People of Georgia* remain vital. For the urgent problems of the 1990's loom larger, and seem even more insoluble, than those of the 1970's, and our people seem more divided than they have been at any time in their history. It seems to me we have two transcendent problems. First, we have lost "something to believe in." That "something" was once faith in religion, human perfectibility or science and technology—tarnished idols all. The absence of a cohering confidence has contributed to our second problem. We have also lost a sense of community. Everywhere we seem divided by contention, while unifying local traditions are assaulted by a vulgar, homogenized mass-market culture. An honest look at our history can help us to restore a shared idealism, valuing the best and accepting the worst in our shared past. Thus informed, we could more easily forgive ourselves and others for our weaknesses and mistakes—past, present and future. Had our people and our leaders such wisdom, Americans would be less self-righteous and more at peace with themselves and the world.

Frank Cunningham's son, Heard County, April, 1941.
Jack Delano, Library of Congress

1. Georgians and Englishmen

THE first colonists sailed to Georgia in November, 1732. The *Gentlemen's Magazine* reported the historic departure: "The *Anne* Galley, of above 200 Tons, is on the point of sailing from Deptford for the new Colony of Georgia, with 35 Families, consisting of Carpenters, Bricklayers, Farmers, etc. who take all proper Instruments. The Men are learning Military Discipline of the Guards, as must all that go thither, and to carry Muskets, Bayonets and Swords, to defend the Colony. She has on board 10 Ton of Alderman Parson's best Beer, and will take in at the Maderas five Ton of Wine, for the Service of the Colony. James Oglethorpe, Esquire, one of the Trustees, goes with them to see them settled." On the *Anne*, according to one of several conflicting reports, there were forty-four men, twenty women, twenty-five boys and seventeen girls, including a potash maker, two merchants, five carpenters, two wig makers, two tailors, a miller and baker, a writer, a surgeon, one gardener, five farmers, an upholsterer, a basket maker, two sawyers, an apothecary, a vintner, a wheelwright, one stocking maker and a reduced military officer. Aboard ship these colonists slept in thirty-five wooden cradles, one for each family, divided by canvas curtains. Every Thursday and Sunday the colonists were fed pork and peas; every Saturday, stockfish and butter; and every other day, beef and pudding. On calm days the lower decks were washed down with vinegar. The women knitted and sewed, while the men exercised at small arms.

20

James Oglethorpe, the founder of Georgia, c. 1735.
A. E. Dyes after Willem Verelst, National Portrait Gallery, London

A Plan representing the Form of Setling the Districts, or County Divisions in the Margravate of Azilia.

During the preceding fifty years, since the last American colony, Pennsylvania, had been chartered in 1681, there had been much talk of new American settlements. Spain had established camps in Florida and what would later become Georgia during the sixteenth century, nearly a hundred years before the first permanent British settlement at Jamestown. When Ponce de León discovered Florida in 1512 he may have come as far north as Georgia; in 1540 Hernando de Soto probably marched across the Georgia frontier; in 1562, French Huguenots under Jean Ribault paused at the coast of Georgia long enough to name some Georgia rivers Seine, Somme, Loire, Garonne, Gironde and Grande; and in 1566 Spanish missions were established on Saint Catherine's and Cumberland islands. In 1713 Thomas Coram, who would later become a Georgia trustee, proposed a "Georgia" which he would have located somewhere between Maine and Nova Scotia. In 1717 Sir Robert Mountgomery, a proud Scot baronet and self-styled genius, designed "Azilia," a feudal barony to be planted on territory that would later become Georgia. But, like Coram's scheme, this was a paper fantasy. In 1724 Jean Pierre Purry of Switzerland appealed to European monarchs to make their colonies a haven for persecuted Protestants throughout Europe, and in 1730 he received a grant from the English Crown to settle on the Carolina side of the Savannah River. In 1729 Joshua Gee proposed sending convicts, vagrants and other useless people who could not support themselves to the border of the southern colonies, where they could buttress the frontier defenses and support themselves on the land, perhaps by raising silk. In 1730 Sir Alexander Cumming brought back to England several Cherokee chiefs from the headwaters of the Savannah River, focussing attention on the unsettled, disputed land between English Carolina and Spanish Florida. Early in 1730 the Board of Trade had been planning an extension of Carolina beyond its southern border, then the Savan-

In 1717 Sir Robert Mountgomery proposed a feudal barony with a turreted fortress on territory that would later become Georgia. *From Mountgomery's* Discourse Concerning . . . a New Colony *(London, 1717), Library of Congress*

nah River. The general notion was that a new English colony in America should be a frontier settlement near Carolina or the West Indies settled by poor people, soldiers or foreign Protestants.

In 1729 a committee of the House of Commons was investigating the condition of several of England's debtor prisons and proposed reform legislation which led to the release of some thousands of prisoners. Inspired by that experience, the committee's chairman, James Oglethorpe, approached another member of the committee, John Viscount Percival, with the idea of sending one hundred vagrants and poor children under the age of sixteen, bound as servants to invalid soldiers, to some place in "the West Indies"—by which he meant anywhere in British America or the Caribbean. "That worthy Gentleman Mr. Oglethorpe opened to me a scheme he had formed, to which I was before a perfect stranger but which I very much supported," wrote Percival, "to settle a hundred miserable wretches, lately relieved out of jail, on the continent of America, and for that end to petition His Majesty for a grant of a suitable quantity of acres, whereon to place these persons." As Oglethorpe, Percival and their philanthropic friends—who later became the Trustees of Georgia—drafted a petition to the King, they adopted many of the ideas about colonies which had been circulating in popular conversation. Oglethorpe had been a veteran of war with Spain, so he recognized that the new colony would become a defense for Carolina from her enemies, especially the Spaniards in Florida. England's poor and foreign Protestants could find refuge in the new colony, which would become a buyer's market for raw materials and a seller's market for manufactured goods. England would no longer have to import silk from France, flax and linen from Russia, wine from Madeira: all would be produced in Georgia. In 1732, King George II, convinced that the venture would be good politics as well as good works, granted the vacant lands lying between the

The Parliamentary committee investigating Fleet Street
Prison in 1729, with its chairman, James Oglethorpe.
William Hogarth, National Portrait Gallery, London

Saltzburg.

Lauffen.

Dirmaning.

Ehedessen müsten wir auf festen Lande bauen,
Nun aber Leib und Vieh dem Wasser anvertrauen.
2

In Gottes Nahmen wird die Reise angetreten,
Jedoch mit frohem Muth u: eifrig=Herzens=belen.
3

Die Lieb Gottes brandt zwar in unsern Herzen,
Doch macht die eüssre Kält, auch eüsserliche
Schmerzen.
4

Braunau.

Obernberg.

Damit die Edle Zeit vergeblich nicht hin striche,
War unser Lust gespräch von Gottes Gnade Reiche.
6

Die Kälte plagt uns sehr, weil sie nicht war zu meide,
Nun Gott gab doch Gedult, die selbe zu erleiden.
7

Der Trost war das sich bald die Schiffahrt werde enden,
Wie es dan auch geschach, am Ufer an zu länden.
8

Passau.

Noch grösser würd der Danck, da Gott es ließ gelin,
Da die zu Passau uns auf freundlichste empfing.
10

Und thaten uns viel guts, auch sonderbahre weise
Daß wir erquickt zu Land fortsetzen unsre Reise.
11

Die Güter, und wer sonst zu Fuß nicht kunte gehe,
Die würden ganz bequehm, mit führen wohl ver=
sehen.
12

Nimwegen.

Rotterdam.

Insul Cassand

In Holland eine Stadt, man nennet sie Nimwegen,
Ward Krancken, u: Gesund, erquickt mit grossem Se=
gen.
14

Die Reise so mit Gott ist worden vor genomen,
Vergnügt uns, da wir sind in Holland angekomen.
15

Sie freisten sich mit uns, u: wir zu gleich mit ihnen,
Gott gebe das sie uns, wir ihnen stützlich dienen.
16

Elias Bock a.H. scit. et excudit Aug. Vind.

Dürenberg.

Burghausen.

Instatt.

Was wir von Dürenberg zur Reiß mit nehmen können,
Wird man nebst Gott vertrauen ja niemand uns.
missgönen.
1

Die würd Temperiert mit Beten und mit Singen,
Da man nebst diesem auch ließ Feuer in Schiffe brin=
gen.
5

Da wir das feste Land mit Freudigkeit betraten,
So danckt und lobten wir, des Höcste Wunderthäte.
9

Savannah and the Altamaha rivers, extending from the Atlantic Ocean westward indefinitely to the South Seas, to a group of trustees for twenty-one years and gave it the benefit of his name, Georgia.

This last and poorest of the thirteen colonies was launched by the most elaborate promotional campaign in early American history. Propagandists painted a rosy picture of what they called "the most delightful country of the universe," a land watered with noble rivers, stored with useful minerals, abounding with beasts, birds and fish to an incredible degree of plenty. The trustees suggested that Georgia lay at the same latitude as the Garden of Eden and the Promised Land. The poets invited Britannia to view a sprightly scene of industry and prosperity: "Instant at work a thousand hands appear / These fell the trees, and these the fabricks rear / The vigorous axe resistless wins its way / And bids th' eternal woods admit the day / The sunny hills afar, and prostrate plains / Invite the labours of the lusty swains / Their annual stores already seem possest / And future harvests wave in ev'ry breast." The future visitor to Georgia would witness a panorama of pastoral plenty: "Let him see those who are now a prey to all the calamities of want, living under a sober and orderly government, settled in towns, which are rising at distances along navigable rivers; Flocks and herds in the neighbouring pastures, and adjoining to them plantations of regular rows of mulberry trees, entwined with vines, the branches of which are loaded with grapes; Let him see orchards of oranges, pomegranates, and olives; In other places extend fields of corn, or flax and hemp. In short, the whole face of the country changed by agriculture, and plenty in every part of it." Phillip Thicknesse recalled his coming to the colony in 1736: "The truth was that I had been so poisoned by the glaring colours in which Oglethorpe had in his printed books displayed the prospects of his new colony of Georgia, that I was determined to go thither. This project had filled me with

Among the persecuted and impoverished colonists recruited for Georgia were the Salzburgers, the exiled Protestants of Austria. *Elias Bach, Royal Library of Denmark*

OVERLEAF:
The Trustees' propaganda suggested that it would be easy to cultivate and settle the rich lands of Georgia. *From Benjamin Martyn's* Reasons for Establishing the Colony of Georgia in America *(London, 1773)*, *Library of Congress*

infinite delight, for I then considered myself as one setting out to begin the founding of a new world." "In a word," wrote Joseph Fitzwalter, another of the early colonists, "I take it to be the promised land."

The trustees promised to transport poor people to Georgia and support them with cattle, land and supplies until the first harvest. In the colony there was to be a public store full of all the tools and provisions the people would need. Each colonist was to receive for equipment a watch coat, a musket and bayonet, a hatchet, a hammer and handsaw, a shod shovel or spade, a broad hoe, a narrow hoe, a gimlet, a drawing knife, an iron pot, a pair of pothooks and a frying pan. Each colonist was to receive for food 300 pounds of beef or pork, 114 pounds of rice, 114 pounds of flour, 114 pounds of peas, 44 gallons of strong beer, 64 quarts of molasses for brewing more beer, 18 pounds of sugar, 5 gallons of vinegar, 30 pounds of salt, plus 12 quarts of lamp oil and 12 pounds of soap. These charity colonists were to have possession of fifty acres of land in Georgia, including a small house lot in town, a garden in the city common and a distant 45-acre farm in the woods. In return for this charity, the colonists agreed to follow the trustees' orders to work at communal labor for the first year and to stay in Georgia for at least two more years. The trustees also offered to grant up to five hundred acres to independent colonists who would come to Georgia at their own expense with at least one servant for every fifty acres of land.

The trustees' promotional campaign attracted a cosmopolitan complexion of colonists to Georgia. The first 114 colonists were followed by five hundred more during the first year and by some five thousand more hopeful people during the next decade. Petitions were sent to the trustees from Rotterdam, The Hague, Genoa and other places where persecuted people had paused in search of permanent asylum. Some Lutherans, exiled by the Catholic archbishop of Salz-

Flying to Georgia in an airship propelled by wild geese, from Grady's *Description of the Famous New Colony of Georgia* (Dublin, 1734). *University of Georgia Library*

The ship *London Merchant*, carrying the Salzburgers, passed the white chalk cliffs of the Isle of Wight as it began the voyage to Georgia in the fall of 1735. *Drawing by Philip G. F. von Reck, Royal Library of Denmark*

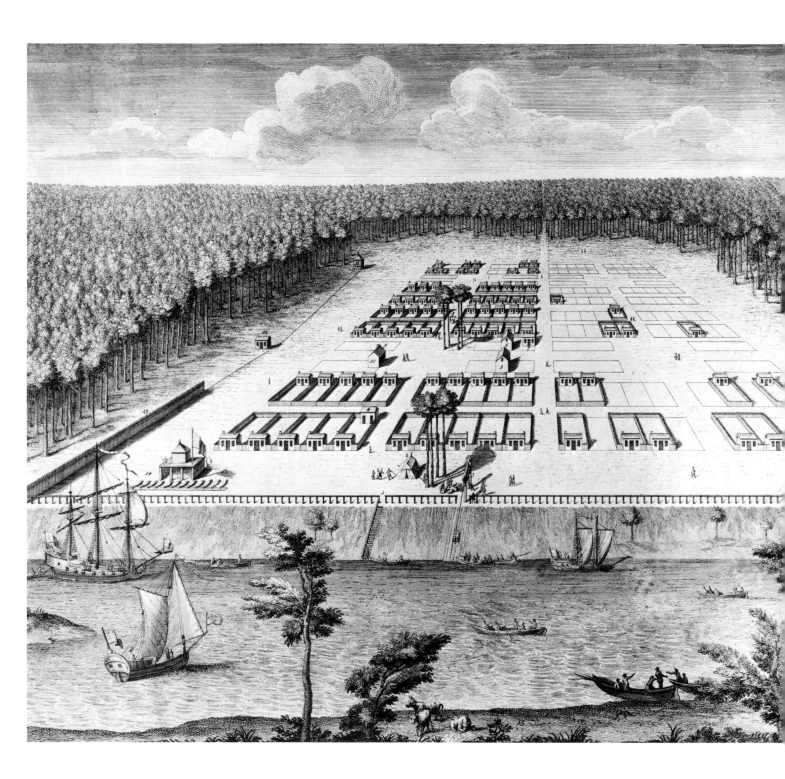

A View of Savannah, a small village on the sandy river bank, surrounded by endless pine forests, March, 1734. *Engraving after Peter Gordon, Library of Congress*

burg in 1731, had already gone to Maryland and Virginia, and Swiss Protestants had settled on the Carolina side of the Savannah River at Purrysburg in December, 1732. In March, 1734, seventy-eight Lutherans came to Georgia and settled twenty-five miles upriver at Ebenezer. Between 1735 and 1738 some forty-five Germans of another Protestant sect, the Moravians, arrived. In January, 1736, the Scot Highlanders, fleeing the abortive Jacobite rebellion of 1715, founded New Inverness, later called Darien, on the Altamaha River. During the colony's first ten years the trustees sent to Georgia at their expense 1,847 colonists, of whom 1,008 were British people and 839 were foreigners. In Georgia, a visitor could hear Gaelic spoken at Darien, German at Ebenezer, French at Highgate, Spanish at Hampstead, Creek among the Indians in the forest.

The first colonists reached the new settlement of Savannah in early February, 1733. Oglethorpe reported to the trustees from the place: "I went myself to view the Savannah River. I fixed upon a healthy situation about ten miles from the sea. The river here forms a half moon, along the South side of which the banks are almost forty foot high and on top flat, which they call a bluff. Ships that draw twelve foot water can ride within ten yards of the bank. Upon the river side in the center of this plain, I have laid out the town." On top of the steep, sandy bluff, the colonists hastily pitched four tents. Except for the cries of birds in the woods, the movement of lazy alligators on the muddy banks of the river and smoke from the campfires of a nearby Indian village, the scene was still, silent and undisturbed.

At the northern end of the bluff, Oglethorpe found a trading house of John and Mary Musgrove, who became invaluable interpreters, and a scraggly Indian village called Yamacraw, about forty Creek Indians recently reduced by smallpox. Mark Catesby, a pioneering naturalist who had come in 1722 to territory which would later become Georgia, reported that these Indians had good teeth and sweet breath, since he had been "necessitated to sleep with them." Phillip Thicknesse, who came to Georgia in 1736, acknowledged that the Indians were gentle and civilized men, no matter how singularly savage their "rude dress, painted faces, sliced ears, nose bobs! and tattooed skin rendered their external appearance to us Britons." Sixteen-year-old Thicknesse purchased the pleasures of an Indian squaw for the price of a pair of boots, some paint, a looking glass, a comb and a pair of scissors. By 1737 a young ensign in Oglethorpe's regiment counted four hundred half-breed children in Georgia. In May, 1733, Oglethorpe signed a formal treaty with fifty chiefs of the Lower Creek Nation. In May, 1734, Oglethorpe returned to England, carrying with him the Yamacraw chief Tomochichi, his nephew Toonahowi and other noble savages from the new world. Colonial agents found little difficulty securing enough land from the Indians, and later treaties of 1763 and 1773 gave the British a further considerable territory that makes up about one-eighth of present-day Georgia.

Military discipline stamped Savannah and Georgia with stern regimentation. On the bluff of the Savannah River, Oglethorpe organized his town to face emergencies, just as any good field commander would plan temporary encampments to preserve order, control and discipline among his troops. The town was laid out in four wards, each made up of four tythings. Each ward was run by a constable to whom four tythingmen reported for the welfare and good conduct of the families in each tything. Ten men in each tything were ready to bear arms at all times and, until other colonists arrived, they would take turns standing watch every fourth night. Oglethorpe inspired good marksmanship by putting up wild turkeys as targets, which then became prizes for the best shot. He gave muskets to orphan boys, so they would become accustomed to habitual guard duty and

The chief of the Creek Indians at Savannah, Tomochichi, with his nephew Toonahowi, c. 1735. *Mezzotint after Willem Verelst, Private Collection*

47.

Senkaitschi, a Yuchi chief, 1736. *Drawing by Philip G. F. von Reck, Royal Library of Denmark*

become good soldiers. Savannah was to be protected by a circle of fortifications, each manned by ten families, and these settlements were established during the first months around Savannah. In December, 1735, Oglethorpe planted a frontier military garrison at Frederica, a village of huts thatched with palmetto leaves and a fort faced with sod, on Saint Simon's Island.

During the first year the new outpost at Savannah was laid out, forty houses were built and a municipal government of courts and magistrates was organized. The colonists were busy clearing land, cutting timber and planting corn, peas and potatoes. In March, 1733, colonist Thomas Causton wrote his wife from the place where Savannah was rising: "It is impossible to give a true description of the place because we are in a wood, but I can't forbear saying it is a very pleasant one." By mid-March two clapboard houses were built and three sawed houses were framed, also a crane to lift heavy loads over the bluff, a battery of cannon and a magazine. By June there were nine framed houses and a smith's forge. Georgia's first houses were the simplest clapboard cottages, raised on log foundations. Thomas Causton, storekeeper at Savannah, described them: "Of one floor, only a cock-loft over it sufficient to hold two beds, the lower part will make one large room and two smaller ones." Francis Moore, recorder at Frederica, described them: "A frame of sawed timber, 24 by 16, floored with rough deals, the sides with feather-edged boards unplaned and the roof shingled." The colonists built a log jail, a well twenty feet deep and a gloriously large oven. The river bluff was fenced, new stairs were built up the sandy bluff. At Tybee Island, a lighthouse, twenty-five feet wide and ninety feet high, was begun, constructed of pine and cedar. Savannah was fortified by a stockade of pine logs, eighteen feet high, facing the forest, and by a battery of twelve cannon, facing the sea. In July the colonists met to name the wards and squares of their little city. By January, 1734, Oglethorpe reported that there were already 437 people receiving the trustees' support in Georgia. Phillip Thicknesse settled on an isolated spot four miles from Savannah, where he shot squirrels and wild birds, bartered venison from the Indians and ate that meat dipped deep in honey. He wrote his mother happily in November, 1736: "The country seems to agree with me very well, for every coat and waistcoat I have is so much too small for me that it will not button within four inches, and I am grown tall and tanned with the sun." Altogether it was, Thicknesse wrote rapturously, "a true Robinson Crusoe line of life!"

The trustees had selected as colonists weak people who were the least able to face the adversities of frontier life. Skidaway Island was settled by a peruke maker, a clogmaker, a ropemaker, a weaver, a dyer, a victualler, a bookbinder and an ex-soldier, most of them city-slickers. Though perhaps no more than a dozen debtors came to Georgia, the trustees were flooded with applications from self-acknowledged failures in England, and the trustees had expressly designed to select only those applicants who were not useful at home and who could not support themselves in England. In January, 1733, the trustees interviewed eight carpenters and found them "miserable objects most of them: One had by sickness been obliged to sell his bed, and another was to sell his tools to pay his creditors." In July, 1733, there were further interviews: "Persons noted down for a future embarkation, reduced to the last extremity of want."

The first colonists on the *Anne* were surprisingly old men 35–50 years of age, evidence that they had decided to resort to Georgia in middle age after early disappointment and failure. William Stephens, secretary of the colony after 1737, characterized the colonists as "poor unfortunate men, who were render'd incapable of living at

The Trustees of Georgia, with a delegation of Indians, a bear
cub and eagle from America. *Painting by Willem Verelst,
The Henry Francis duPont Winterthur Museum*

home . . . a parcel of poor people." Samuel Penseyre, who fled to Georgia to escape from his bitchy, drunken wife, knew very well how "Nobody would leave his native country if they had not some crosses or misfortunes to bear."

The colonists found themselves in a strange land of alligators, deer, snakes, bears, bugs, sandy beaches and palm trees. The climate was hotter than expected: an eighteenth-century visitor, La Rochefoucauld, complained that he could cook an egg in just twelve minutes by putting it into the Georgia sand on a hot summer day. The climate was colder than expected: William Stephens, who came to Georgia to report to the trustees in 1737, said ice formed in the chamber pot under his bed on cold winter nights. Thomas Causton wrote his wife in 1735: "Every insect here is stronger than in England. The ants are half an inch long and, they say, will bite desperately." Edward Kimber, who came to Georgia in 1743, reported "an abundance of torments, as Cock-roaches, Wood-ticks, Sand-flies, Moskettos, and other Vermin." Francis Moore in 1736 said that the alligators at Frederica were "terrible to look at, stretching open an horrible large Mouth, big enough to swallow a man, with rows of dreadful large sharp teeth, and feet like dragons, armed with great claws."

The charity colonists had agreed to accept elaborate prescriptions in return for the trustees' benevolence, a smothering paternalism that would weigh heavily on the colonists in Georgia. A typical colonist who had been shipped to Georgia at the trustees' expense had to be twenty-one years old, so he could be strong enough to plow his land and carry a musket. He had to agree to remain in Georgia for at least three years, so he could contribute to the stable defense of the place. He had to agree to plant one hundred white mulberry trees on every ten acres of his land to feed silk worms—a Georgia industry which never materialized. He could claim no more than fifty acres of land, so the population would not be too spread out. He could not sell or mortgage his

"MacDonnel, Piper to the Highland Regiment . . . Tried in the Tower for Desertion in June 1743 [and] sent to Georgia" by John Bowles. *Private Collection*

The first houses built by Englishmen on Saint Simon's Island were a tent-like hut of cruck construction and another of puncheons or upright logs buried in the ground, 1736. *Drawing by Philip G. F. von Reck, Royal Library of Denmark*

42 land and only his son could inherit it. He could not purchase slaves, because they might overturn the government or create inequality among the settlers. South Carolina, which had three times as many blacks as whites in 1734, was considered weak and unstable. The Georgia colonist could not drink rum, which would lead to weakness and indolence. The idea behind all these restrictions was what Oglethorpe called "the Agrarian Equality," by which he meant the design of building a population of small farmers capable of supporting and defending themselves.

These benevolent, aggravating regulations made ambitious and propertied colonists frustrated and unhappy. They could see how Carolinians owned and sold their land, not merely had possession of it, how they profited from slave labor, drank rum and joined in the lucrative molasses and timber trade with the West Indies. Ships stayed away from Georgia because people were too poor to buy a shipload of merchandise and could not afford to hire labor and then ship cheap raw materials which competed with those produced by slave labor. There was no cash in the public store in 1737 to pay workers building a fort at Savannah, so the project was abandoned. At different times there were no munitions, physicians, candles, meat or money at Savannah. In February, 1737, hunger was so great that people began stealing vegetables from neighbors' gardens and the trustees' cattle were killed secretly in the woods at night. Distracted by their obligations to perform communal labor, building their houses and fighting the Spaniards in Florida, the colonists were not able to support themselves, and the trustees' subsistence, intended for only the first year, had to be extended indefinitely until the public store was closed in 1738.

In Oglethorpe's absence there was dispute instead of leadership in the colony. Thomas Causton, the storekeeper, was accused of

A. Haupt Straßen. B. Marckt Plätz.
rer ein jeglicher Zehen Wohnunger
welcher ebenfals eingezaint. P. Holl
Land wo die Saltzburger ihre Vieh

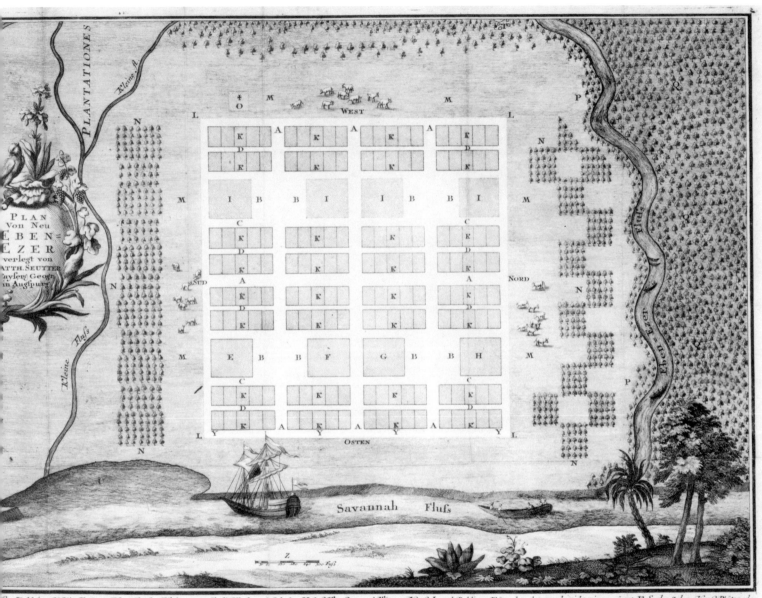

en. D kleine Gäßlin. E. Store Häuß. F. Pfarr-Wohnungen. G. die Kirchen u. Schulen. H. daß Wayßen auch Witwen Häuß. I. auch Publique Plätz aber dato noch nicht eingezaümet. K. Sechs Zehen Häuß Plätze, de
einem Häuß Hof u. Garten bestehet. L. ein Schindel Zaun Sechs Fuß hoch welcher sehr gut steht, u. von ferne der Statt ein ansehen macht als wäre sie verpalysaliert. M. Vieh Weyde. N. Gärten. O. der Kirch Hoff
onlichs Land einer kleinen Nation Indianer. R. die Mühl. S. Hübricorn ein Dorff. T. Alt Eben-Ezer zwey Stund von dem Neuen Eben-Ezer. U eine See. W. Purysbury zwey Stunden von Eben-Ezer. X hohes
Y. Sind 20 Häuß Plätze zwischen drey Strassen, so Hr. General Ogleth, für nach komende Vornehme u. Reiche Leuthe aufbehalten. Z. Maaß Stab von 300 Fuß wornach der Plan der Statt ausgemessen

In February, 1736, the Salzburgers began building the town
of New Ebenezer, some ten miles north of Savannah near
the Savannah River. A 1747 engraving after Matthew Seut-
ter. *Library of Congress*

starving the people and enriching himself. The workmen at Tybee in 1735 were said to be continually drinking instead of building the lighthouse. John Wesley, the minister at Savannah, was run out of the colony, accused of improper relations with one of his communicants, Sophia Hopkey. In 1735 a group of unhappy indentured servants and others conspired to overthrow Savannah and murder the magistrates. Paul Amatis, the silkman, came to Savannah in 1734, found the trustees' garden with trees and stumps where he should have seen carefully tended rows and weedless furrows, and he threatened to shoot Joseph Fitzwalter, the public gardener, if he ever tried to return. There were gossips, horse stealers, cattle rustlers, jail breakers, counterfeiters and murderers among the first people of Georgia. Alice Riley drowned weak old Mister Wise in a bucket of water. Mrs. Bland who came from Charleston in 1735 was considered to be quite mad. Joseph Watson, the Indian trader, would run around drunk and lie naked with the Indians. Some colonists lived openly with mistresses and had bastard children, like Thomas Christie and his housekeeper who shared only one bed "which they made use of together." Brides at Purrysburg in 1734 were suspected of being ready to bear children in less than the usual nine months, "whether by reason of the fruitfulness of the Air or of some Tryal of Skill beforehand." John Terry wrote Harman Verelst, the trustees' accountant, in 1741: "I long very much to get out of Savannah, for there are here Human Snakes, much more dangerous than the Rattle ones."

The vocal malcontents in the colony complained that Georgia's prospects had been misrepresented in England, that the land restrictions were a hardship for people without sons and that prosperity would never come to Georgia without slaves. When two representatives of the unhappy colonists, Peter Gordon in 1735 and Thomas Stephens in 1739, tried to present these complaints in person before

Oarsmen, women with waterbuckets on their heads, men offering handshakes and the first houses at New Ebenezer in the spring of 1736. *Drawings by Philip G. F. von Reck, Public Record Office (top), Royal Library of Denmark (bottom)*

the trustees in London they were dismissed unsympathetically. From their office in Old Palace Yard, Westminster, and warm suppers at the Castle Tavern, the trustees could not appreciate the real hardship of life in Georgia. The trustees felt unfairly maligned by ungrateful people. Peter Gordon wrote what he thought the trustees wanted to hear, when he warned that the idle colonists in Georgia might "return like a dog to his vomite, to gratify those vicious habits of idleness & drinking, which brought them to that unhappy state before." The trustees believed that the colonists were men who had been useless in England and who were again useless in America. The prohibitions against slaves and rum, proposed and drafted by Oglethorpe, reflected the trustees' belief that the colonists were weak and needed a healthy dose of discipline. When Oglethorpe, a stern disciplinarian, was asked what laws were intended for Georgia, he reportedly replied, "Such laws as the Trustees think proper, what business have poor people to do with laws?"

Oglethorpe returned to Georgia in September, 1738, with five transports of nearly seven hundred soldiers and a commission from the King as Captain General of the combined forces of South Carolina and Georgia. He discovered that there had been no money for months to pay the soldiers and sailors at Frederica. He faced a mutiny of soldiers at Fort Saint Andrews on Cumberland Island, during which the general was himself grazed by a bullet. Oglethorpe journeyed to Savannah and dismissed many of the public officers and, finding the colony nearly bankrupt, closed the public store. In October, Spain and England declared open war. In November, Oglethorpe reported sarcastically the gloomy situation of the colony: "I am here in one of the most delightful situations as any man could wish to be. A great number of debts, empty magazines, no money to supply them, numbers of

George Whitefield's Bethesda Orphan House, outside Savannah, 1740–42, was the largest and most famous building of early Georgia, seen in a promotional tract by the evangelist. *Library of Congress*

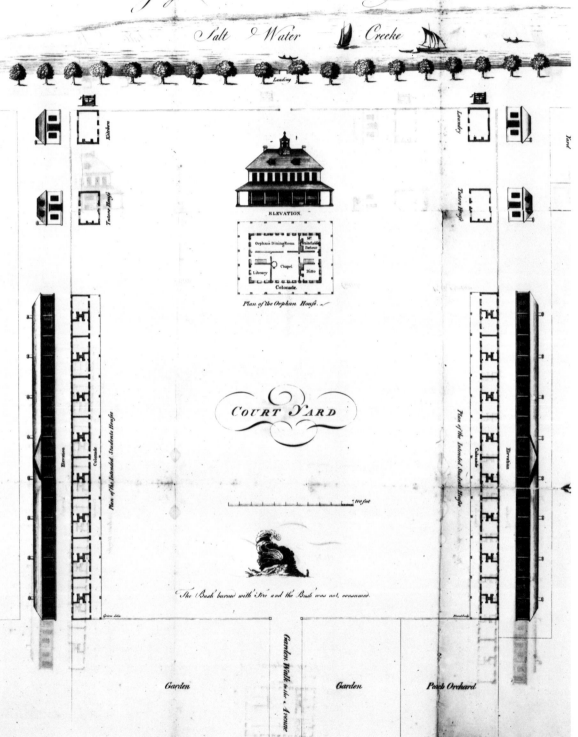

The Plan and Elevation of the Present and Intended Buildings of the
Georgia ORPHAN HOUSE & Academy

Salt & Water Creeke

Landing

Kitchen

Laundry

Yard

Tutors House

Tutors House

ELEVATION.

| Orphans Dining Room | Mr Whitefields Parlour |
| Library | Chapel | Ditto |

Colonade.

Plan of the Orphan House.

Elevation

Colonade

Plan of the Intended Students House

COURT YARD

Plan of the Intended Students House

Colonade

Elevation

100 feet

The Bush burned with Fire and the Bush was not consumed.

Garden

Garden Walk to the Avenue

Garden

Peach Orchard

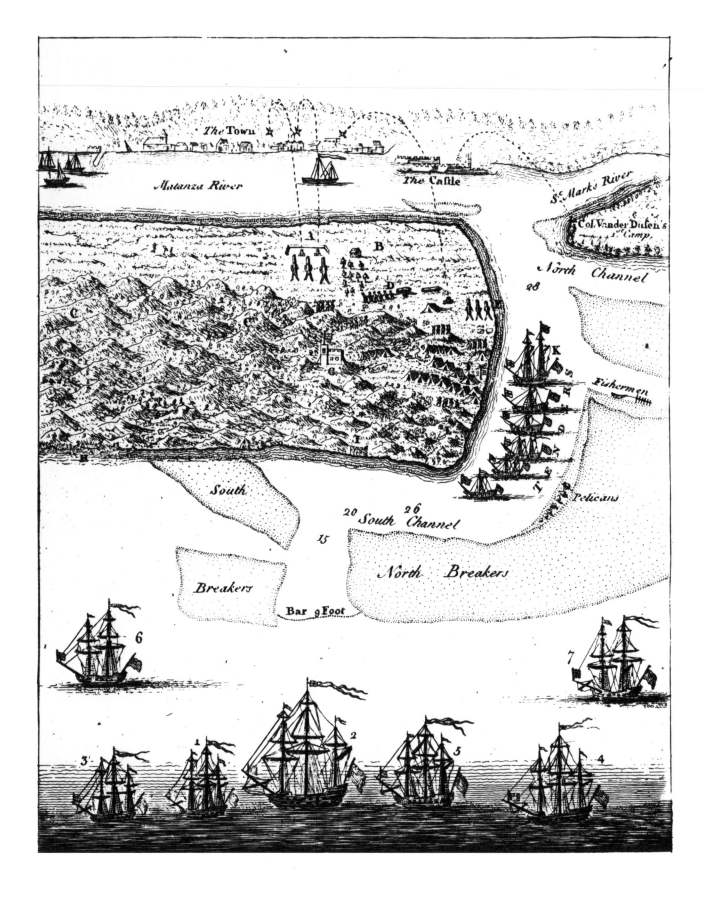

The Town

Matanza River

The Castle

St Marks River

Col. Vander Dusen's Camp

North Channel

B

D

C

28

K

Fishermen

I

Pelicans

H

South

South Channel

20

26

15

Breakers

North Breakers

Bar 9 Foot

6

7

3

1

2

5

4

people to be fed, mutinous soldiers to command, a Spanish claim and
a large body of troops not far from us."

In November, 1739, the Spaniards fell on Amelia Island and
killed two Georgians. In retaliation Oglethorpe marched into Florida,
ravaging the countryside. During the winter of 1740 Oglethorpe collected nine hundred British troops and eleven hundred Indians for an
attack on Saint Augustine. Two Spanish forts, Diego and Moosa,
capitulated, but the great fortress of Saint Augustine withstood the
British assault. The Georgians did not receive the prompt support
expected from Carolina, the attack was delayed long enough for
Augustine to receive reenforcements and the hurricane season was
approaching. So Oglethorpe abandoned the siege in July, 1740. In
May, 1742, a Spanish armada, sailing from Havana to Augustine,
launched an invasion of Georgia. In July at Bloody Marsh on Saint
Simon's Island, the Georgians repulsed the Spaniards within only a
mile of Frederica. In March, 1743, Oglethorpe made another unsuccessful advance on Augustine.

The general's aggressive behavior, establishing Frederica and
southern forts beyond Georgia's chartered limits, had provoked the
Spaniards to retaliate and imposed a great economic burden on the
Georgia colonists. Men who were needed to support the colony were
drawn off to fight in Florida. When strange, swarthy men appeared
from the woods or privateers appeared on the horizon, men were
called from their fields to face frequent false alarms. Facing impending
invasion in February, 1737, the alarmed citizens of Savannah raised an
uncontrollable clamor for a new and stronger fort to which they might
flee in the last extremity and all productive work was stopped while it
was being built. In 1737 the common at Savannah was still littered
with logs and cluttered with weeds, evidence of neglect and unfinished
work. By the summer of 1738 only one quarter of the plantations in the

In 1740 General Oglethorpe, in a reckless defense of Georgia's southern border, marched his army into Florida and
attempted without success to capture the Spanish citadel of
Saint Augustine. *A view by Thomas Silver in* London
Magazine *of 1740,* University of Georgia Library

vicinity of Savannah had been cleared. In the summers of 1740 and 1742 the terrified women and children of Savannah evacuated their town, and the public records were shipped to more remote Ebenezer for safekeeping.

The inhabitants of the colony were dispirited and heartbroken. Elisha Dobree wrote from Frederica in February, 1737: "When people are driven to poverty, distress or expectation of, they will drink to get up their courage. For we always have observed that the people in England will either be quite forlorn without hopes or mad with liquor. Our people are almost mad and I am obliged to drink with them." In August, 1740, Henry Garrett wrote: "I got into a very bad corner of the world, where poverty and oppression abound to such a degree that it's become proverbial this way to say 'as poor as a Georgian'." Unhappy Georgians realized that by crossing the Savannah River and entering Carolina they could get the land, slaves, peace and prosperity missing in Georgia. Between 1737 and 1741 the population of Georgia may have dropped from five thousand to only five hundred. In 1741 there were only 80 people left at Darien and 161 civilians at Frederica. In 1742 there were 287 people at Savannah. When Oglethorpe's regiment was disbanded in 1749, of more than 650 soldiers and their families, only 151 decided to remain in the colony. From their refuge in Charleston, the Georgia malcontents cried bitterly: "The inhabitants of Georgia are scattered over the face of the earth, her plantations a wild, her towns a desert, her villages in rubbish, her improvements a by-word, and her liberties a jest; an object of pity to friends and of insult, contempt and ridicule to enemies!"

Many people believed that Georgia was a miserable corner of the world not worth saving. There was talk in Parliament in 1741 of making Port Royal in Carolina the southernmost extent of Britain's "plantations" in America and retreating. Sir Robert Walpole considered re-

St. Paul's Church at Augusta, a center of Indian trade established in 1736, seen in the builder's drawing in 1749. *Society for the Promotion of the Gospel, London*

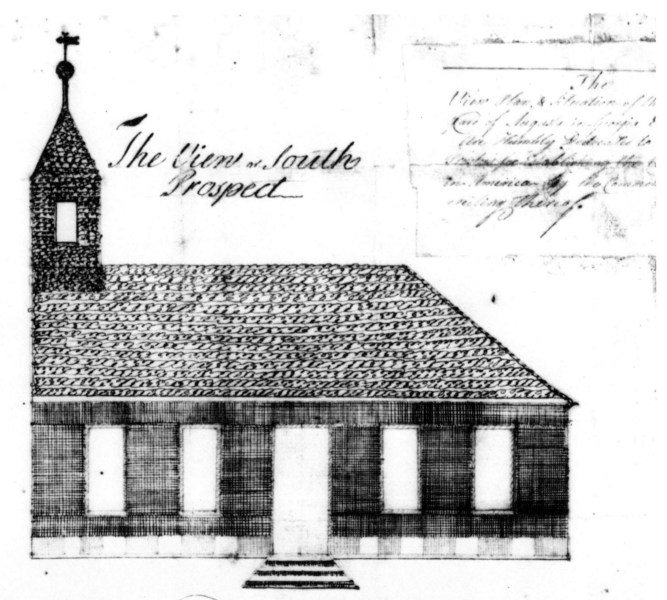

The View or South
Prospect

The
View Plan, & Elevation of the
Care of Augusta in Georgia &
are Humbly Dedicated to
Society for Establishing the &
in America by the Commiss
ercting thereof.

The Frame of the Church is of Wood So Strong that it will last for many Years between
the Studs is a Wall of Clay Eight Inches thick, Supported in the Center of that Clay with
pieces of Wood three inches thick, let into the Studs by a Groove. The Outside is rough
cast with Lime & Gravil appearing like Stone, The inside Plaistered white wash'd and
arch'd the roof Supported by two Columns as p Plan which we propose to have
handsomely Ornamented. We do likiwise, when we are able, intend to underprop
the Church with Brick, as it appears by the Plan but at present it is only Supported
with loggs of lasting Oak, which is the only part that does not answere the View.

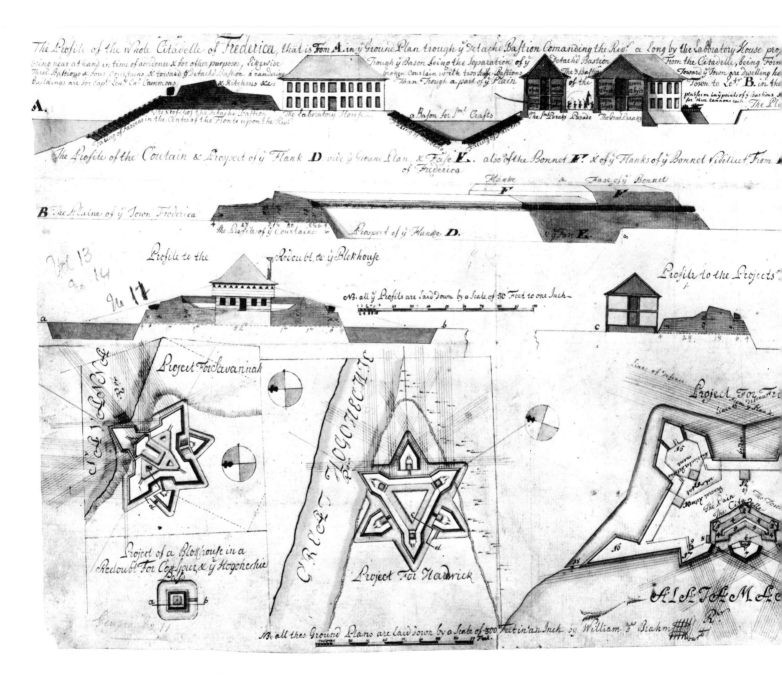

Under the able, stable administration of Georgia's Royal governors, plans for fortifications at Savannah and along the coast were prepared by the military engineer William De-Brahm, c. 1761. *Public Record Office, London*

turning Georgia to Spain as a peace offering. There was slack attendance at Georgia trustees' meetings: "It is a melancholy thing to see how zeal for a good thing abates when the novelty is over and when there is no pecuniary reward," Oglethorpe's friend Egmont wrote. In 1742 for the first time Parliament refused to vote money for Georgia, and Egmont resigned as a trustee in unsuccessful protest. In July, 1743, Oglethorpe sailed back to England, saying farewell to the colony he had founded. John Dobell wrote bitterly to the trustees in July, 1743: "There is such an odium cast upon Your Honours and the scheme you have formed for the colony that both you and it are detested by all!"

Georgia's second decade was an anticlimax after the colony's exhausting, exciting early years. There were further threats of Spanish invasions during 1744 and 1745, for the war with Spain did not end until 1748. Some people continued to expect Oglethorpe to return and rescue the colony, but he finally married in 1744 and settled down to a comfortable literary life. Meetings of the trustees were held very seldom after 1744–45. The land inheritance restrictions had never been strictly enforced, in 1742 the act prohibiting rum was repealed, and in 1750 the slave prohibition was also revoked. In 1750, the trustees allowed a provincial assembly to convene in the colony.

In 1751 Parliament again refused money to the Georgia trustees. In June, 1752, the trustees surrendered their charter to the King. They had sent to Georgia about twelve hundred British people and one thousand foreigners and spent £153,000 of public and private money. Two-thirds of the charity colonists had eventually left the colony. Perhaps six thousand people came to Georgia in the 1730's; probably all but one thousand had left by 1743. By 1752 there were still only two thousand whites and one thousand blacks in Georgia. Military preoccupations had made the early colony an unhappy and unsuccessful endeavor. The province, a mere pimple at the southern extremity of the British empire in America, was not a very significant project compared with the great wars taking place in Europe. Georgia could not be, in the words of the trustees' promotional slogans, both a Garden of Eden and the Gibraltar of America. Great expectations had led to great disappointments in Oglethorpe's Georgia.

John Reynolds, the first of three governors appointed by the King to govern Georgia before the Revolution, reached the colony in December, 1754, and found the province miserably poor. Savannah, he wrote, was a mere village of 150 houses, "all wooden ones, very small, & mostly very old," and the Savannah River was blocked with sunken wrecks and old trees. Frederica was "entirely in Ruins, the Fortifications entirely Decayed and the Houses falling down." At Augusta only a ruined wooden fort remained, "so rotten that great part of it is propt up, to prevent its falling." When the governor and his council tried to meet for the first time to transact business, the government building collapsed at one end, forcing them to retreat to a shed behind the courthouse. Governor Reynolds estimated the colony's diminished population to be 4,500 whites and 1,855 blacks in 1755. In July, 1757, the colonial assembly summarized the distressed condition of Georgia: "To find ourselves in a Country surrounded with most cruel & insolent Savages; absolutely destitute of every means of defending ourselves from their barbarities in case of a Rupture; without any Forts that are not utterly in ruins or funds to erect them; Without any Troops stationed here save twenty odd Rangers yet unestablished, unpaid & undisciplined; without any Vessels of War for the protection of our Coast; with but few Inhabitants & those poor & widely dispersed over the Province; open on one Side to every possible insult from the most inconsiderable of the Enemy's Vessels: In such a situation our all is precarious!" Life in the colony continued unhappy under Reynolds,

The entrance to the Savannah River was marked by a wooden lighthouse and protected by a small fort on Cockspur Island, seen in anonymous drawings dated December, 1764. *University of Georgia Library*

The Royal governors who administered the colony after 1752 spent most of their time negotiating with the Creek Indians, whose settlements are seen in William Bonar's 1757 "Draught of the Creek Nation." *Public Record Office*

an arrogant man who played favorites in the provincial government and who was removed from office in 1756.

Georgia made considerable and rapid progress under the squireship of Henry Ellis, governor between 1757 and 1760, and James Wright, governor after 1760. After its idiosyncratic beginnings as a charitable trust, Georgia was now cradled in the lap of the British imperial system. Georgia was governed by a royal governor and council appointed in England and by a Commons House of Assembly elected by the colonists. After 1750, slaves had been allowed in the colony, and Georgia's first slave codes were passed in 1755 and 1765. In 1758 the Anglican church became the established religion of the colony, and Georgia was divided into eight parishes, administrative units christened with religious names—Saint Paul (Augusta), Saint George (Waynesboro), Saint Matthew (Ebenezer), Christ Church (Savannah), Saint Philip (Hardwick), Saint John (Midway), Saint Andrew (Darien), Saint James (Frederica). In 1763 James Johnston, Georgia's first printer, established the *Georgia Gazette*, the first newspaper published in the colony. In 1763 the Treaty of Paris, ending the Seven Years' War, compelled Spain to cede Florida to Britain, removing the greatest threat to the tranquility and prosperity of Georgia.

Significantly, the Georgia governors spent most of their time approving land grants and greeting Indians, whom James Wright called "most Troublesome, disagreeable & Expensive Guests." Always there was the threat that Cherokees and "frenchified" Creeks would become allies of the French colonials in Mississippi and Alabama against the English in Georgia and Florida. The decade of the 1760's became a period of border barbarities between eager settlers and embattled Indians. For every enemy scalp they would bring in, Governor Ellis in 1760 promised the Indians a trading gun, three pounds of powder, six pounds of shot, a blanket, a pair of boots and a four-gallon keg of rum. Indian presents ordered from England included nests of tin kettles, tin pots, looking glasses, checked shirts, striped shirts, ruffled shirts, cloth, knives, hats, coats, razors, scissors, ivory combs, hatchets, brass wire, trading guns and fowling pieces, best and common flints, saddles and bridles, paint, gunpowder and bullets, bags of tobacco. A great conference of Creek, Cherokee, Choctaw, Chickasaw, Catawba Indians and provincial governors from Georgia, the Carolinas and Virginia was held at Augusta in 1763 and succeeded in opening up to settlement nearly two and one-half million acres of Indian land, lying between the Oconee and the Savannah rivers in the northwest and between the Altamaha and Saint Mary's rivers in the south, tripling the size of the colony. In 1773 Governor Wright offered to assume debts owed by the Indians to white traders, in return for a "New Purchase" which added two million more acres in the northwest. Altogether Wright succeeded in adding some six million acres of land to the one million inherited from the trustees in 1754.

Early in the 1760's the first tide of transcontinental migration reached Georgia. The end of the Spanish war opened the southern coast near Florida for settlement, and the establishment of slavery encouraged ambitious, substantial people to come to Georgia for the first time. Along the coast, a group of Puritans from Connecticut and Massachusetts, who had lived for more than a generation in South Carolina in the early eighteenth century, settled in 1752 at Midway, a place "midway" between the Savannah and Altamaha rivers. In 1761 they established Georgia's second port, Sunbury, a city of great promise in the eighteenth century. The lands at the southern border of Georgia were becoming so attractive that the government of South Carolina tried to claim the territory south of the Altamaha River, arguing that King George II had granted to Georgia's original trustees only lands stretching to that place and no further south. Both Governors

The Three Cherokees came over from the head of the River Savanna to London 1762
Their Interpreter that was Poisoned.

The Royal governors negotiated Indian treaties that
opened to settlement one-eighth of present-day Georgia.
These Cherokee chiefs were brought to London in 1762.
University of Georgia Library

The emerging merchants and planters of Georgia pros-
pered under the Royal governors and were, like the Tan-
natt family of Savannah seen here in 1770, deeply divided
by pre-Revolutionary agitation. *Painting by Henry Ben-
bridge, The National Gallery of Canada, Gift of Jasper
H. Nicholls*

Ellis and Wright considered shifting the capital of Georgia from Savannah to a new city farther south, Hardwick. Some 160 Germans under William DeBrahm settled at Bethany, west of Savannah, in 1751; in 1768 Irish Protestants settled at Queensbury on the Ogeechee; in 1768 Quakers from North Carolina settled at Wrightsboro, north of Augusta. In 1761 Governor Wright complained that the colony was already being overrun with "a Parcel of Runagates from Virginia & North Carolina, a kind of Vagrants who live like the Indians by Hunting & Stealing other Men's Cattle & Horses." By 1761, 394,944 acres of land in Georgia had been granted to new settlers. From three thousand whites and two thousand blacks in 1754, Georgia's population swelled to fifty thousand people, half free and half slave, by the end of the Revolution.

The able, stable administration of the royal governors, the pacification of the Indians and the opening of their lands to white settlement, the expansion of plantations and slavery along the coast and up the Savannah River, the end of the Spanish war and the flood of immigration into the southern frontier were all leading Georgia to prosperity for the first time. Rice, wheat and indigo were the main crops, and there was a busy trade in provisions, lumber and naval stores. In 1754 the colony exported 1,899 tons of goods worth £15,744 on 9 square-rigged vessels and 43 sloops and schooners; in 1770, the colony exported 10,514 tons of goods, worth £99,383 on 83 square-rigged vessels and 113 sloops and schooners. In 1755, 2,200 barrels of rice had been shipped from Savannah; in 1768, 17,783 barrels were exported. In 1762 Georgia exported 417,783 feet of timber, 325,477 staves and 683,265 shingles; in 1772 the colony exported 2,163,582 feet of timber, 988,791 staves and 3,525,930 shingles, an increase of five hundred percent in ten years. With good justification then, Governor Wright reported with sanguine confidence in December, 1768, that Georgia was at last making "a very rapid progress toward being an Opulent & Considerable Province."

Still Georgia was a young and weak colony, whose areas of settlement extended, at the deepest point, only some thirty to fifty miles inland from the Atlantic coast and along the banks of the Savannah River. Of the one and one-half million people who lived in the American colonies in 1760, fewer than ten thousand lived in Georgia and thirty-six hundred of those were slaves. Inevitably, this little colony was more dependent on England than the older and richer northern settlements. The provincial government and the colonists shared a common interest in making Georgia a prosperous and contented place. James Wright, who owned nineteen thousand acres of Georgia land, twelve plantations, five hundred slaves, was the natural leader of the new class of rice planters and shipping merchants.

All the good works of the governors had, however, contributed to the wealth, self-confidence and ambitions of Georgia's merchants and planters. The provincial assembly, composed of some twenty-five prominent planters, traders and professionals, began to assert its prerogatives during the 1760's. In 1767 the assembly refused to provide barracks and other necessities for the British soldiers stationed in Georgia. In 1768 the assembly disobeyed instructions from the governor, endorsed a circular letter from northern colonies protesting against the Townshend Acts, which imposed import duties on the American trade, and Governor Wright dissolved it. During 1771–72 the assembly three times elected Noble Wimberly Jones, a famous radical, as its speaker against instructions from the governor, who again dissolved it. In 1774 the assembly claimed the exclusive right to nominate Georgia's colonial agent to England. But these were political contests, unclouded by complicating moral issues, for Governor Wright was always a popular man and he did not have the resources

George Washington, when he visited Savannah in 1791, stayed at Stephen Miller's house, built c. 1785–90, seen in a 19th-century view. *Georgia Historical Society*

Less than a handful of pre-Revolutionary buildings has
survived in Georgia, and most of these have been altered.
Charles Oddingsells Cottage, Savannah, 1798–99.
Frances Benjamin Johnston, Library of Congress

with which to threaten the Georgians. During the 1760's and early 1770's, conservatives tended to be officials and clergymen from England, older and wealthy Savannahians, Indian traders, recent immigrants, the Germans at Ebenezer, all those who were most dependent on Britain; and radicals were younger Savannahians, frontiersmen and residents of two southern coastal parishes. Noble Jones and James Habersham were conservatives, while their sons Noble W. Jones, James Habersham, Jr., and John Habersham were radicals. In Georgia, where there were no moral controversies, it is easy to understand how the Revolution was a political struggle among the Americans.

At best reluctant rebels, Georgians were led toward revolt by pressures and propaganda from outside the colony. In 1765 the Stamp Act was passed by Parliament to provide income for imperial defense by requiring that legal documents and publications be written or printed on special paper sold by public officials. Georgia was so far away from the center of action that the stamped paper did not reach Savannah until a month after the tax was to go into effect. But Georgians' objections were so weak that the stamps were used to clear vessels for about two months, one of the rare instances of the use of the stamps in America. South Carolina voted to stop all trade with Georgia in retaliation. Georgia sent no delegates to the Stamp Act Congress, held in October, 1765. In December, 1773, Bostonians dumped a shipload of tea into their harbor rather than allow it to be landed and taxed. In the spring of 1774 the port of Boston was closed, protest meetings were held in Savannah during July and August, 1774, against these "intolerable acts" by Parliament. In 1774 the northern colonies resolved to boycott British manufactures and organize a nonimportation association, which Georgia was reluctant to join. Again South Carolina voted to cut off trade with Georgia and Rhode Island, the only two colonies still trading with England. Two Georgia parishes on the southern coast—Saint James and Saint Andrew—adopted that Continental Association independently at the end of 1774, and Saint James tried to secede from Georgia and join South Carolina. Georgia sent no delegates to the First Continental Congress, held at Philadelphia in September, 1774. A Georgia provincial congress in 1774 was attended by representatives from only four of Georgia's eight parishes, reflecting widespread public apathy; and the three delegates elected by that assembly to attend the Second Continental Congress declined to serve, saying they could not speak for a majority of the province.

During the year 1775, however, revolutionary sentiments spread through Georgia, as rumors and reports filtered south from other colonies, and mobs began to flout public law and demonstrate the weakness of royal officials at Savannah. In February, a crowd of some twenty people outside Savannah, costumed as sailors and with their faces blackened, tarred and feathered a guard who was protecting some goods seized by the government for nonpayment of duty. In May news reached Georgia that a sanguinary battle had taken place at Lexington, Massachusetts, between rebels and redcoats, and the public magazine at Savannah was robbed of six hundred pounds of gunpowder. In June the first liberty pole was set up at Savannah. In July a second provincial congress met at Savannah, this time attended by 102 delegates representing all but two of Georgia's eight parishes. Joachim Zubly, a Presbyterian minister from Savannah and member of the Continental Congress from Georgia, expressed his colony's sentiments of 1775: "I shall briefly state the immediate causes that have given rise to this Provincial and a general American Congress: To enforce some Acts for laying on a duty to raise a perpetual revenue in America, which the Americans think unjust and unconstitutional, which all America complains of, and some provinces have in some measure opposed. A fleet and army has been sent to New England, and after a long series of hardships by that province patiently endured, it is

George Spencer House, Savannah, c. 1791. *Frances Benjamin Johnston, Library of Congress*

New Englanders began to immigrate to the Georgia coast
in the late 18th century, among them settlers from Connecticut and Massachusetts who built a Congregational
Church at Midway about 1792. *Carolyn Carter*

now out of all question that hostilities have been commenced against them; blood has been shed, and many lives have been taken away; thousands, never as much as suspected of having any hand in the action which is made the pretence of all the severity now used against that province have been and still are reduced to the greatest distress. How far and wide the flame so wantonly kindled may be permitted to spread, none can tell. . . . The Americans have been called 'a rope of sand,' but blood and sand will make a firm cementation, and enough American blood has been already shed to cement them together into a thirteen fold cord, not easily to be broken. . . . My Lord, the violence of the present measures has almost instantaneously created a continental union, a continental currency, a continental army. . . . The most zealous Americans could not have effected in an age what the cruelty and violence of administration has effectively brought to pass in a day."

Four provincial congresses were elected between July, 1775, and June, 1777. These became Georgia's first revolutionary government, electing Archibald Bulloch the first president and delegating to a Council of Safety the power to act when the provincial congress was not in session. The Council of Safety collected and purchased provisions and war materials, bribed and negotiated with the Indians, improvised taxes and elections, raised and spent money, censored the newspapers and did all the everyday business of a functioning revolutionary government until May, 1777, when the state's first constitution went into effect. In June and September, 1775, regular shipments of gunpowder to the Indian traders were captured at the mouth of the Savannah River and some of it, according to tradition, was dispatched to aid the Continental Congress and was used at the battle of Bunker Hill. In July the revolutionaries in Savannah removed stores, cannon and powder from the royal magazine, while the governor and his loyal councillors watched powerless to stop them. During the summer, the rebels took control of the provincial militia by electing their own officers sworn to revolutionary loyalty, and Wright was helpless to punish or resist the street mobs. In August, a crowd forced open the royal jail and freed a man who had been imprisoned for recruiting troops for a Carolina regiment. In September, Governor Wright lamented: "It is really a Wretched State to be left in . . . the government totally annihilated and assumed by Congresses, Councils and Committees, and the greatest Acts of Tyranny, oppression, gross Insults Committed and not the least means of Protection, Support or even Physical Safety." In December armed men occupied the Savannah courthouse and royal law enforcement was abandoned.

In January, 1776, the governor wailed that with "No Troops, no Money, no Orders, or Instructions and a Wild Multitude gathering fast, what can any Man do in Such a Situation?" Almost immediately Wright was arrested, but, breaking his parole, he escaped to the H.M.S. *Scarborough*, a man-of-war anchored in the Savannah River, during February and returned to England. In July, the Continental Congress at Philadelphia adopted the Declaration of Independence, signed by Georgia's three delegates, Button Gwinnett, George Walton and Lyman Hall. In May, 1777, a new constitution went into effect, replacing the old colonial parishes with counties named for English politicians who had supported the American cause—Wilkes, Burke, Effingham, Glynn, Chatham, Camden, plus one named for the ideal cause of Liberty. In late 1777 Loyalists were expelled from the state. The military situation remained quiet in Georgia during 1777 and 1778, except for intermittent invasions by English Loyalists who had taken refuge in Florida and for three unsuccessful American expeditions against East Florida and Saint Augustine. Meanwhile, the British were busy concentrating their forces in New York, New Jersey and Pennsylvania.

But in 1778 Sir Henry Clinton, British commander in America, decided to mass an expedition of some twenty-five hundred to thirty-

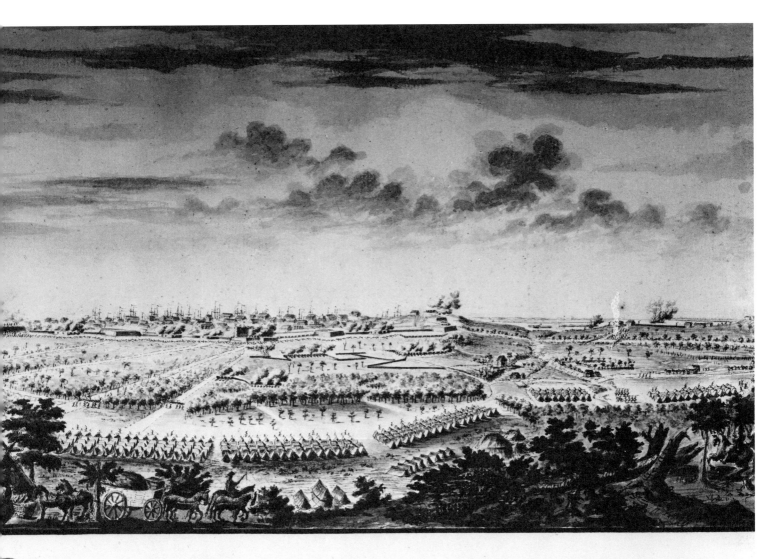

de Savannah, du Camp, des Tranchées et de L'attaque Octobre 1779.

In October, 1779, French and American forces attacked Savannah, which had been held by the British since December, 1778. The attack failed, and Savannah and much of the Georgia coast remained in British hands until 1782. *Drawing by Pierre Ozanne, Library of Congress*

five hundred troops under Archibald Campbell to recapture Georgia. This force reached the southern coast in December, 1778, and recaptured Savannah easily when a slave showed the British a secret passage behind the American lines. Then General Augustine Prevost, commander at Saint Augustine, brought forces from Florida, recaptured Sunbury and occupied Savannah, while Campbell's army captured Augusta. In March, 1779, the British government was restored in territory occupied by the King's forces, and Governor Wright returned to Savannah during the summer and continued to administer his part of Georgia until July, 1782.

The British controlled Savannah and the area about forty miles around it, and the rebels controlled the interior and lower coast. The American Congress was too poor to fortify Georgia after 1778 and the British were preoccupied with military problems in Florida and the Carolinas. In the backwoods of Georgia, the Revolution settled into a guerrilla war. William Lee, who moved to Georgia in 1780, found that there was no safety in the countryside, for both loyalists and rebels were plundering and killing all who joined the opposite party. In February, 1779, a rebel militia under Andrew Pickens, John Dooly and Elijah Clarke defeated redcoats at Kettle Creek. In March, Lieutenant Colonel Mark Prevost, brother of Augustine Prevost, massacred rebel troops at Briar Creek. In October, 1779, a French fleet of twenty-two vessels and four thousand soldiers, commanded by Charles Henri Comte d'Estaing, attempted to recapture Savannah from the British. After a four-day bombardment and a furious direct assault, in which Sergeant William Jasper and Count Casimir Pulaski were mortally wounded, the Allies were compelled to abandon the siege and retire in humiliation. During 1780–81 the important fighting in the South was between Cornwallis and Greene in the Carolinas, and two governments, rebel and royal, continued to govern Georgia until the Peace of Paris in 1783.

James Oglethorpe, aged 102, sketched from life at the sale of Dr. Johnson's books in 1785 by P. Ireland. *Private Collection*

2. Indians and Settlers

AFTER the Revolution Georgia was one stage for the American epic of exploration across a virgin land, the mass migration of eager settlers into Indian territory and the creation of a new society deep in the wilderness. King George II had granted the colonial trustees an immense domain which extended from the Atlantic Ocean indefinitely to the South Seas, and until 1802 the new state of Georgia continued to claim lands stretching to the Mississippi. Even after the state surrendered its western claims to the United States, Georgia remained the largest state east of the Mississippi, some sixty thousand square miles, about the same size as England and Wales. During the debates at Philadelphia in 1787 to revise the Articles of Confederation, Georgia's delegates voted for a strong central government, because they wanted national help to fight the Indians, and voted with larger states for the concept of unequal representation in the new national union, because they expected Georgia to become a rich and populous state someday.

But before 1800 the only part of Georgia which had been populated was a narrow strip of settlement along the Atlantic coast and up the Savannah River to Augusta, perhaps no more than fifty miles deep at most. Georgia was still a vast, virgin land, possessed by deers, panthers, wolves, bears, polecats, wildcats, buffaloes, elks, turkeys, eagles and Indians. William Bartram, who came to Georgia in 1773, described sylvan scenes of enchanting innocence: "A vast expanse of

After wandering through the Southern colonies during the Revolution, William Lee, seen here in his Indian dress in 1780, settled in Georgia. *From Lee's* True and Interesting Travels *(York, 1782), University of Georgia Library*

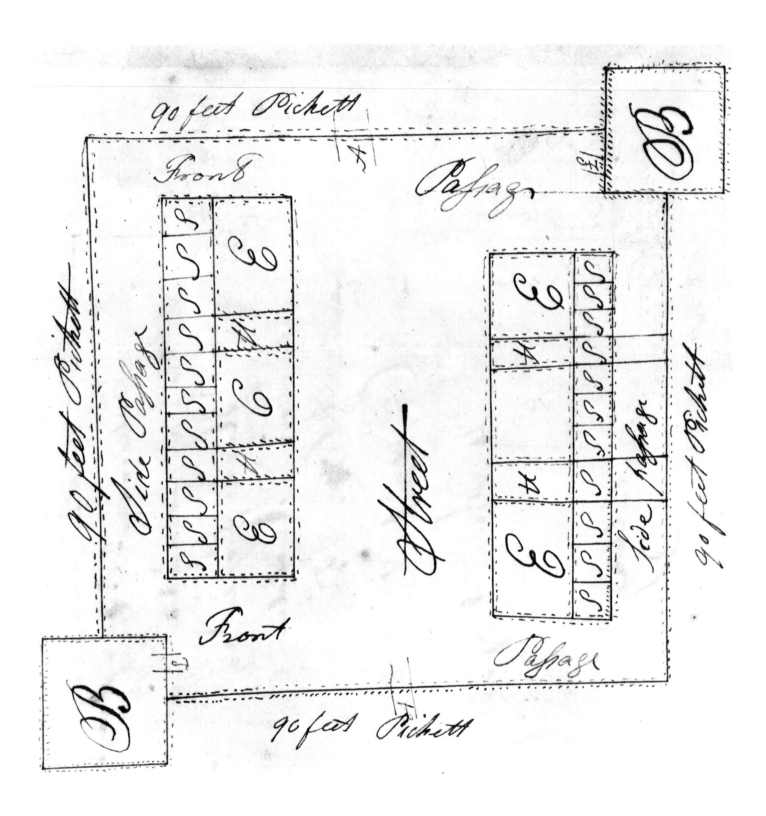

The plan of a frontier stockade presented by the builders
Isham Williams and Thomas Kemmerley in 1797. *Georgia Historical Society*

green meadows and strawberry fields; a meandering river sliding through, saluting in its various turnings the swelling, green turfy knolls, embellished with parterres of flowers; flocks of turkeys strolling about them, herds of deer prancing in the meadows or bounding over the hills; companies of young, innocent Cherokee virgins, some busy gathering the rich fragrant fruit, others having already filled their baskets, lay reclined under the shade, disclosing their beauties to the fluttering breeze, and bathing their limbs in the cool fleeting streams." Bartram recognized, with the rare historical insight of a man who loved universal nature more than the British empire of which his native Philadelphia was then a part, that this formerly secure and tranquil scene was now threatened by a torrent of invading settlers.

At the very time Bartram was in Georgia, during the 1770's, a wave of immigrants, settlers from North Carolina and Virginia, began to move into the state, forced south because tobacco farming had exhausted the soil of their old homesteads. The Indians called all the strangers on their lands "Virginians," signifying that these were new men from outside the state, not merely old Georgia colonists moving into the interior from the coast. All three signers of the Declaration of Independence from Georgia were born outside of the state: George Walton, born in Virginia, came to Georgia in 1769; Button Gwinnett, born in England, came to Georgia in 1765; Lyman Hall, born in Connecticut, came to Georgia in 1756. An army of Virginians came to fight in Georgia during the Revolution and remained there. Georgia granted land after the Revolution to nine thousand veterans, of whom only two thousand were native Georgians. Abraham Baldwin, the founder of the University of Georgia, was a Connecticut man and a graduate of Yale College, after which the new Georgia university was modelled. A North Carolinian who came to the new state in 1782 wrote home: "Georgia must in a few years be one of the Richest States in the Union,

Two Revolutionary veterans from Virginia who claimed lands in Georgia in the 1780's, Oliver Porter and his brother, seen in a silhouette by Francis Chapman. *Georgia Department of Archives and History*

and Where I've no doubt you may live happy and secure a lasting and Valuable Estate for your self & family." Even before John Pope reached Augusta in 1791, he had already heard that a great proportion of the people who lived there were "insolvent Refugees from the northern states." James Jackson wrote John Milledge in 1797: "Some thousands of people are now moving into this State. They will rush like a torrent in search of subsistence." Between 1790 and 1800 the population of Georgia nearly doubled, from 82,548 to 162,686, and by 1820 the state counted 340,989 people.

The old, established society of coastal Georgia, settled generations earlier by direct colonization from England and closely tied to her still by commercial and personal relations, viewed the new up-country settlers with much disdain and some fear. James Habersham of Savannah wrote in August, 1772, of these new immigrants along the northern frontier of Georgia: "I have lately received Advice from Mr. Barnard of Augusta, that several idle People from the Northward, some of whom, he is told, are great Villains, Horse Stealers, etc. have settled and built Hutts on the Lands proposed to be ceded by the Indians to His Majesty, and that more might be expected to join them, and if not drove off and they should be suffered to encrease, it might here after be attended with Difficulty to do it. The present Intruders, I am informed, are Persons who have no settled Habitations, and live by hunting and plundering the industrious Settlers, and are by no Means the sort of People that should settle these lands . . . idle and disorderly Vagrants." During the Revolution, the low-country plantations had been devastated and the government run by British soldiers, while the up-country people had run their own insurgent government. In 1783 Anthony Stokes, former chief justice of the colony, reporting on the condition of the British plantations at the time of the Revolution, wrote: "The Southern colonies are overrun with a swarm of men from

Scenes of hunting and dancing in frontier Georgia, a child's sketchbook, 1793. *Georgia Department of Archives and History*

40

April the 11 day Anno Domini 1793

The Hunter and the Buck &c

Two women and the Bear, April 12 day 1793

the western parts of Virginia and North Carolina, distinguished by the name of Crackers. They are the most abandoned set of men on earth, few of them having the least sense of religion. When these men are routed in the other provinces, they fly to Georgia, where the winters are mild, and the man who has a rifle, ammunition, and a blanket, can subsist in that vagrant way which the Indians pursue; and as the Indians dwindle away before them, they certainly threaten ruin to the civilized parts of the rice colonies." The earliest political contests in Georgia came between the party of James Jackson, William Crawford and George Troup, expressing the view of property owners from the coast and settlers from Virginia, and the party of John Clarke and later Wilson Lumpkin, representing the poorer settlers from North Carolina.

It was, recalled James Lamar, whose family moved from Augusta to then remote Columbus during Georgia's frontier settlement, "a time when to move was in the blood of everyone." Augusta Harris Hansell, born at Thomasville in 1817, remembered that her relatives suffered from the same nomadic itch and were "always ready to sell out and move on the frontier, being fond of the rather wild and often dangerous life of those living close to the warlike tribes of Creek indians." Gideon Lincecum's father spent thirty years wandering back and forth between South Carolina and Georgia, finally settling in Texas: "My father loved a border life, and the place he had purchased on the Ocmulgee, as the people had already commenced settling on the opposite side of the river, was no longer looked upon as a border country. He sold his place and was soon equipped and geared up for the road, and so was I. I had been reared to a belief and faith in the pleasure of frequent changes of country, and I looked upon the long journey, through the wilderness, with much pleasure." Charles Lyell in 1845 recorded how a middle Georgia farmer complained of "a want of

A camp by moonlight near Fayetteville, 1819–21.
Aquatint by Shaw and Hill, New York Public Library

elbow room," although his nearest neighbor was six or seven miles distant. John R. Vinton, sent on a mission to Georgia by President Adams and the Secretary of War in 1827, found himself "amidst a rude homely people, full of pride & high-toned republicanism."

The Georgia frontier beyond the area of established plantations was being overrun by caravans of land-hungry men, most of them before the 1830's small farmers from the northern states. Gideon Lincecum recalled such a journey, another relocation across the western frontier of Georgia into Alabama in 1818: "The journey, the way we travelled, was about five hundred miles, all wilderness; full of deer and turkeys, and the streams were full of fish. We were six weeks on the road; and altogether it was, as I thought and felt, the most delightful time I had ever spent in my life. My brother Garland and I 'flanked it' as the wagons rolled along and killed deer, turkeys, wild pigeons; and at nights, with pine torches, we fished and killed a great many with my bow and arrows." The Augusta *Chronicle* described a similar migration in 1819: "Passed through this place from Greenville District, bound for Chattahoochee, a man and his wife, his son and his wife, with a cart but no horse. The man had a belt over his shoulders and he drew in the shafts—the son worked by the traces tied to the end of the shafts and assisted his father to draw the cart, the son's wife rode in the cart, and the old woman was walking, carrying a rifle and driving a cow."

Georgia was a tough territory, swarming with drunken, brawling men, who were scrambling and struggling for land. Florida was the refuge of freebooters, outlaws, adventurers, runaway slaves, for it remained Spanish territory until 1819. Alabama was a place where the marauding Indians came from and where the latest line of settlers disappeared to. The South Carolinians always looked on Georgians as crude "westerners." La Rochefoucauld, an exiled peer of France who

A frontiersman, "Mr. Ricks, a native of the interior of the State of Georgia," sketched in his hunting dress by Basil Hall, 1828. *Lilly Library, Indiana University*

Mr Ricks in his hunting dress —
24ᵗʰ March 1820.
A native of the interior
of the State of Georgia

Mr Webb
Emanuel Co[unty]
Georgia
24th March

138

came to Georgia in 1796, called Georgia the worst-regulated part of the Union and her inhabitants the most idle, drunken and disorderly anywhere in the new United States. In 1787 the young wife of a frontier tavern keeper at Washington, Georgia, wrote to her father in distant Massachusetts: "All of the State of Georgia would be no inducement to me to bring my dear little Lambs in this flock of Wolves, as I may properly call many of the inhabitants of this State. The people in general are the most profane, blasphemous set of people I ever heard of. Sometimes . . . they look like a flock of blackbirds, and perhaps not one in fifty but what we call fighting drunk. It is impossible for you to conceive what language is used." At Washington, when parties were held at the log courthouse, this is how they would call out the dances: "Gentlemen, lead out your partners. Them that's got on shoes and stockings will dance the cotillion; them that's got on shoes and no stockings will dance the Virginy reel; them that's got on nairy shoes nor stockings will dance the scamper-down." George Gilmer, an early settler, remembered how his family breakfast depended on someone's catching a 'possum overnight or shooting a rabbit early in the morning. Peter Remsen, a New York trader passing through Milledgeville in 1818, viewed the state legislators at the capital city of Georgia: "Their conduct was beneath that of any crew of sailors that was ever seen. Cursing, quarrelling, hollowing, drinking, getting drunk. Disputing landlords' bills. Drunken men hugging sober ones. Illiterate, mean appearances, readiness for rasseling, etc." Columbus, at the extreme western frontier of Georgia, was especially notorious for its drunken Indians and young prostitutes. It was a world of hunting, drinking, gambling, fighting which A. B. Longstreet captured in his classic *Georgia Scenes*, a volume of stories first published at Augusta in 1835. It was an era which gave Georgia some wonderful place names which evoke the wild frontier—Guinea Nest, Rabbit Trap, Snake Rag, Sugar Tit, Wolf Skin, The Lick, Devil's Half Acre, Red Bone, Hello!

Another frontiersman, Mr. Webb of Emanuel County, sketched by Basil Hall, 1828. *Lilly Library, Indiana University*

Fierce fighting was a conspicuous element of frontier life, invariably noted by Georgia travellers and a reflection of the state's primitive society. The state legislature in 1787 complained against Georgians who would "willfully or maliciously cut out or disable the tongue, put out an eye, slit the nose, bite or cut off the ear, nose or lip, or cut off or disable any limb or member of any person." Charles Wilson Janson came to Georgia about 1807 and observed a gouging match: "We found the combatants fast clenched by the hair, and their thumbs endeavoring to force a passage into each other's eyes, which several of the bystanders were betting upon the first eye to be turned out of its socket. At length they fell to the ground, and in an instant the uppermost sprung up with his antagonist's eye in his hand!!! The savage crowd applauded, while, sick with horror, we galloped away from the infernal scene." Anthony Stokes, Georgia's colonial chief justice, marvelled how a small weakling could disable a lusty, muscular fellow by grabbing his opponent's head, putting a thumb into his eye, strangling his throat and biting his left cheek, all in one swift, dexterous operation. William Butterworth, a young sailor at the Georgia coast before 1830, expecting frontier settlers to fight a classic English boxing match, was horrified at the appearance of the victim of a typical brawl: "A shocking spectacle, part of the skin of his forehead, with his eyebrow, hanging upon his face, and the blood streaming down his cheeks. His antagonist informed me it was bit, assuring me that a quantity of hairs were then sticking in his teeth." Isaac Weld, who came to Georgia in 1798, reported: "Whenever these people come to blows, they fight just like wild beasts, biting, kicking and endeavoring to tear each other's eyes out with their nails. To perform the horrid operation, the combatant twists his fore-fingers in the side locks of his adversary's hair, and then applies his thumb to the bottom of the eye, to force it out of the socket." In some parts of the state, he said, every third or fourth

Sketches by Basil Hall of Joseph Collins, his son George Washington Collins and others of Tatnall County and the "Embryo Town" of Columbus in 1828. *Lilly Library, Indiana University*

Tykes

Sabrina

Mr Joseph Collins & his Son George Washington Collins
Tatnall County — Georgia C.L.
22nd March
1828.

Vol IX
L 147

Embrys Town of Columbus on the banks of the
Chatahoochie in Georgia 31st March 1828
C.L.

Coventry
The Houses in Georgia consist generally of two parts
or wings with an open space between them, covered by one
common roof. There is consequently no outer door
as those for the rooms open from this exposed space, or
passage. Sometimes there are there are two rooms
at each end, but generally only one.

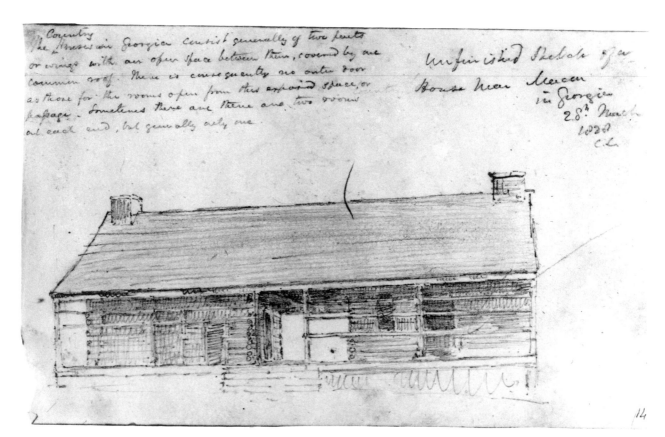

14

River 29ᵗʰ March 1828
C L

144

man appeared with just one eye. Louis Milfort, a supercilious French traveller to the back country about 1780, said that Georgia was the home of a unique race of men, "Anglo-Americans of a peculiar sort, called Gougeurs, who are nearly all one-eyed." At Jacksonborough it was said that in the mornings after drunken frolics and fights you could see the children picking up *eyeballs* in *tea saucers*! In the gold-mining district of north Georgia, when Cynthia Hyde, an American of the Georgia wilds, was brought to trial for assaulting Polly Hefling, the lady declared with passion that she was "as supple as a lumber-jack, strong as a jack-screw, and savage as a wildcat."

When he left the immediate vicinity of Savannah in 1828, Basil Hall was quickly lost: "If required to give the localities with any precision in such a route, it would have been necessary to carry sextants and chronometers in the carriage. For we were fast sinking into the wild and little known parts of the continent, on which the traces of man were as yet but feebly impressed." When Charles Lyell landed on the Georgia coast in the 1840's to hunt fossils, it seemed to him "as if we had been dropped down from a balloon, with our baggage, in the midst of a wilderness." The itinerant minister Francis Asbury wandered among remote Savannah River rice plantations in 1793 and prayed for deliverance: "Oh, how dreadful to be here in the dark!" Places to eat and rest were hard to find and then were generally unsatisfactory. Along the isolated frontier, where there were few public taverns, it was customary for travellers to take room and board in private homes. In 1783 Joshua Clifford instructed his daughter in the fine arts of innkeeping, Georgia-style: "Let your bedsteads be cleansed every March, and you will be seldom troubled by multipedes. Let your water bucket stand so high that your children shall not dabble in it. Keep a spit box in each room: this will teach vulgar people that the floors were not made to spit on. Don't allow your children to examine

Sketches by Basil Hall of a dog-trot house near Macon and a log house near the Flint River, 1828. *Lilly Library, Indiana University*

the baggage of your guests; nor to belch upwind at the table." There were few single beds or private rooms. George Featherstonhaugh wrote with philosophical calm from the Georgia-Tennessee border in 1835: "We stopped for the night at another dreadful dirt hole. The fatigue of the day made me sleep well, although on the floor." Sheets were changed only when they began to smell. Always, Margaret Hall lamented in 1828, there was the usual complement of fleas and bugs: "But we have ceased to expect anything else. Every night I am awakened by Mrs. Cownie striking a light to commence her search for her tormentors. When I undress, I find them crawling on my skin, nasty wretches." James Buckingham summed up the sorry tourist situation at Sparta in 1839: "The dirty state of the room in which the table was laid, the filthy condition of the table-cloth, the coarse and broken plates, rusty knives and forks, and large junks of boiled pork, and various messes of corn and rancid butter, added to the coarse and vulgar appearance and manner of most of the guests, made the whole scene the most revolting we had yet witnessed in the country."

After the Revolution there were just 50,000 citizens of English Georgia, while there were perhaps 35,000 Indians, Creek tribes in the western and southern parts of the state and the Cherokee tribes in the northern parts. The colonial agents had found little difficulty securing enough land from the Creeks, and early treaties made in 1733, 1763 and 1773 gave the English a considerable territory which represents about one-eighth of present-day Georgia. But during the first four decades of the nineteenth century, the population of Georgia swelled from 162,000 to 691,000. From 1800 to 1809, fourteen new counties were created; from 1810 to 1819, nine more counties; from 1820 to 1829, twenty-nine; from 1830 to 1839, seventeen. Milledgeville was laid out at the head of navigation on the Oconee River; later Macon and Columbus were

The dog-trot cabin at Elijah Clarke State Park is a recreation of the most popular house form of the American frontier. *Van Jones Martin*

Travellers' Rest, a tavern outside Toccoa, was built about
1815–25 and enlarged about ten years later. *Van Jones
Martin*

established on the Ocmulgee and Chattahoochee. The state capital was moved from Savannah to Augusta in 1785, to Louisville in 1796, to Milledgeville in 1806, each time farther northwest, following the center of population. The Creek tribes, who had occupied the banks of the Savannah River when Oglethorpe landed, were forced to retreat to the Oconee River in 1802, to the Ocmulgee in 1804, to the Flint River in 1821, to the Chattahoochee in 1826. The Cherokees, living in mountainous north Georgia, where they were less in the way of expanding settlements, were not removed from the state until 1838.

Anthony Stokes reported in 1783 that during the Revolution the Americans lost much of their fear of the Indians, "for the Crackers [the new settlers], who are destitute of every sense of religion, which might withhold them from acts of perfidy and cruelty, have been discovered to outdo the Indians in bearing hunger and fatigue; and as they lead a savage kind of life, they are equally skilled in the arts of bush-fighting, and discovering the enemy by their tracks." If an immigrant were not scalped by an Indian in a dispute about territory, said Stokes, then he would probably be cheated out of his land by "profligate white men called Crackers, who are much addicted to exercise the Rights of Man, when they see a good horse, or any other article they like, having abolished the institutions of their Ancestors, forbidding theft, and other crimes, which the Crackers find it convenient to commit." In 1742 William Stephens called Indian traders "a Parcel of loose debauched Fellows." Benjamin Hawkins, Washington's Indian agent in the South, bluntly characterized some of the white traders he met among the Upper Creeks: "a hard drinker," "an indolent, careless man," "an active man of weak mind, fond of drink and much of a savage when drunk," "an enemy to truth and his own character," "a man of infamous character, a dealer in stolen horses." These men were building trade routes, establishing new settlements and slowly de-

94

priving the Indians of their ancestral hunting lands. La Rochefoucauld in 1796 carped that, in the continual quarrels between the whites and Indians, the settlers were in the wrong four times out of five: "It is admitted by everybody that there cannot be a more vicious set of people than the whites who dwell on the boundaries; they rob, murder and betray the Indians."

The excitement of new opportunities and new lands at the time of the Revolution, a rush to plant cotton lands in middle Georgia during the flush times after the invention of the cotton gin, the scramble for land in northwestern Georgia, after gold was discovered there in 1829, all contributed to the frontier land fever. Samuel Butler, who moved from Virginia to the back country above Augusta in the Broad River Valley in 1784, complained in homemade rhyme: "New Georgia is a pleasant place / If we could but Enjoye it / Indians & Rogues they are so great / But allmost have destroyed it. / Could but the Indians be subdewd / And Rogues could have their portion / There could be no better place / On this side of the ocean." Francis Asbury, that travelling minister who came to Georgia on several tours between 1791 and 1815, observed sadly the disappointing effects of his preaching: "I have ridden about two hundred and fifty miles in Georgia, and find the work, in general, very dead. The peace with the Creek Indians, the settlement of new lands, good trade, buying slaves, etc., take the attention of the people." In 1794 Elijah Clarke, who had led an expedition against the Indians during the Revolution, took unilateral possession of some unceded Creek lands on the Oconee River, constructed forts, settled on soil that had been previously guaranteed to the Indians and proclaimed an independent republic, which he occupied with some land-hungry followers until President Washington ordered the Georgia governor to intervene. In the lawless spirit of the time, the settlers looked on the Indians as trespassers on their own land.

Georgia gold miners, from William Phillips's *Essay on the Georgia Gold Mines* (New Haven, 1833). *University of Georgia Library*

Four of the Creek Indian chiefs who came from Georgia and other Southern states to meet with President George Washington at New York in 1790, sketched by John Trumbull. *Yale University Art Gallery (tl, br) and Smithsonian Institution (tr, bl)*

Bad relations between Indians and settlers in south Georgia were aggravated by troubles in north Florida, seen in this melodramatic "Massacre of the Whites by the Indians and Blacks in Florida," c. 1836. *Library of Congress*

This land fever was stimulated by public policy and private speculation. Georgia, hoping to encourage settlement of her territory, gave away the land virtually without cost. After the Revolution, the state government promised two hundred acres of open land, plus fifty additional acres for each family member, to any American soldier who could produce evidence of his wartime service. The state granted some three million acres of this bounty land to nine thousand veterans. After 1802, the state ran a lottery, and each white male adult citizen was entitled to draw for new land. Between 1803 and 1833 eight great distributions were made, totalling 22,404,250 acres. Speculators bought up and resold much of this land, with advertising which a wag satirized in 1787: "Halloo, Halloo, Halloo. The subscribers will sell on most moderate terms: Ten millions of acres of valuable pine barren land in the province of Utopia, on which there are several very sumptuous air castles, ready furnished, that would make commodious and desirable habitations for the gentlemen of the speculative class." In 1795 four companies acquired a vast territory from the state of Georgia, some forty million acres of what is now Alabama and Mississippi, near the Yazoo River, paying a very small price. It was revealed that all but one member of the state legislature had been bribed in the bargain, a terrific public outcry was raised and the act was rescinded by the next legislature.

During the Revolution the Creeks, although they tried to remain neutral, were forced by an English embargo to fight against the Americans. In the following years, each episode of border warfare ended with further Indian cessions. In 1782 at Augusta and in 1785 at Galphinton, certain Creek tribes ceded lands between the Altamaha River and the Florida boundary to the Georgians. These treaties were disputed by other Indians, led by Alexander McGillivray. In 1786 these tribes made a reprisal raid against the settlers, which provoked the

OVERLEAF:
In 1813 General John Floyd and the Georgia militia from Fort Hawkins attacked and killed some two hundred Indians at Autosse in Florida. *University of Georgia Library*

Georgians to dispatch fifteen hundred militiamen against them. At Shoulderbone the Indians were compelled to accept the two disputed treaties and to cede still more territory. During 1787–89, the Creeks reportedly killed 82 people, captured 30 whites, 110 blacks, 642 horses, 984 cattle and 387 hogs and burned 89 houses. In 1790 President Washington invited Alexander McGillivray to New York, where he was flattered and bribed into accepting a compromise treaty. But this treaty was repudiated by other Creek factions in Georgia led by William Augustus Bowles, a former English soldier who was living with the Indians, and denounced by the Georgians, because the treaty seemed to guarantee indefinitely Indian occupation of some Georgia territory. Georgia proceeded to make its own treaties in 1785 and 1786 with sympathetic factions of the Indians.

In 1802 Georgia traded her western claims to territory of Mississippi and Alabama in return for the United States government's promise to remove all the Indians as soon as possible on reasonable, peaceful terms. Though most of the Lower Creeks in Georgia remained friendly to the Americans during the War of 1812, the Upper Creeks in Alabama took that opportunity to assert their independence. In 1813–14 Andrew Jackson and his Tennessee army, with John Floyd from Fort Hawkins and his Georgia militia, attacked the Creeks at the Georgia border. The Georgians objected that the Treaty of Fort Jackson, which ended this war, left the heart of Georgia—from the Ocmulgee to the Chattahoochee—in Indian possession. In 1823 Georgia Governor George M. Troup condemned the federal government for not removing the Indians, and President Monroe appointed two Georgians as Indian agents. These agents made a treaty at Indian Springs, which ceded all Creek lands in Georgia. But the new President, John Q. Adams, declared the treaty illegal and forbade Georgia's surveying this land. But Governor Troup proceeded to survey the land and even

George Lowery was one of several Cherokee chiefs who petitioned Congress to protect their lands from the avaricious Georgians in 1824. *Painting by George Catlin, Thomas Gilcrease Institute of American History and Ar Tulsa*

to commence preparations for war with the United States. At the last minute, the United States negotiated treaties with the Creeks in Washington during 1826 and 1827, averting war and purchasing the last Creek territory in Georgia.

In mountainous north Georgia, the Cherokee tribes were less in the path of settlement, so there was less pressure to remove them from the state. Tutored by Moravian missionaries from North Carolina, the Cherokees had become a civilized nation, with an alphabet, a newspaper, a written constitution and a capital city at New Echota. In fact, they even owned slaves. But gold was discovered at Dahlonega (the Indian name means "the place of yellow metal") in 1829, and by 1830 some three thousand Georgians were digging for gold in Indian territory. In 1830 the Cherokees sued against the Georgians' violations of Indian rights, but the Supreme Court ruled that the Indians were not citizens and therefore could not apply to the Court. When the Court ruled in another case, brought by an Indian missionary who had been jailed by the Georgians, that Georgia could not extend its laws over the Indians, the Georgia governor, Wilson Lumpkin, stated that his state would ignore the judges, and President Jackson, a determined Indian fighter, did not attempt to enforce the Court's decision. Without any treaty giving them rights to Cherokee lands, Georgians surveyed the Indian territories in 1831, granted them to Georgians in a lottery in 1832, and in 1834 settlers were allowed to take possession and the Cherokees were ordered to get out within two years. In the ensuing confusion, different Cherokee factions accepted, rejected and again accepted a final cession of their last Georgia lands. In 1838 General Winfield Scott and the U.S. Army rounded up the last sixteen thousand Cherokees who remained in Georgia and herded them to the West. The Indians had no horses, they had to march on foot; it was winter, and five thousand of them died.

William McIntosh, a Creek chief, was shot to death by other Indians because he assented to the final cession of Creek lands in Georgia in 1824. *Alabama State Archives*

3. Masters and Slaves

HUMANITARIAN feelings had little to do with the decision to make Georgia the only one of the thirteen colonies which prohibited slavery at its founding. The trustees of Georgia wanted to make their southern outpost strong against Britain's Spanish and Indian enemies, by compelling the colonists to feel a responsibility for productive work, by preventing the development of large plantations financed with cheap labor, keeping the landholdings small, compact and easily defensible and by maintaining a cohesive equality among the settlers. Peter Gordon, one of the first colonists who came to Georgia on the *Anne* in 1733, wrote with unconscious irony: "It is morally impossible that the people of Georgia can ever get forward in their settlements or even be a degree above common slaves without the help and assistance of negroes." In 1743 Thomas Stephens, a vocal malcontent who argued that the prohibition against slavery was another hindrance which had retarded the progress of the colony, complained: "It is clear as light itself, that negroes are as essentially necessary to the cultivation of Georgia as axes, hoes, or any other utensil of agriculture." Only with the adoption of slavery after 1750, and the end of the Spanish war in 1763, did Georgia prosper for the first time. Once they were legalized, slaves became deeply woven into the fabric of Georgia life. In 1751 William DeBrahm, provincial surveyor of the southern colonies, found "scarce three Dozen of African Servants," but by 1771, when he finally

104

Two former slaves, Jack and Abby Landlord, were photographed by J. N. Wilson in Savannah about 1875. *New-York Historical Society*

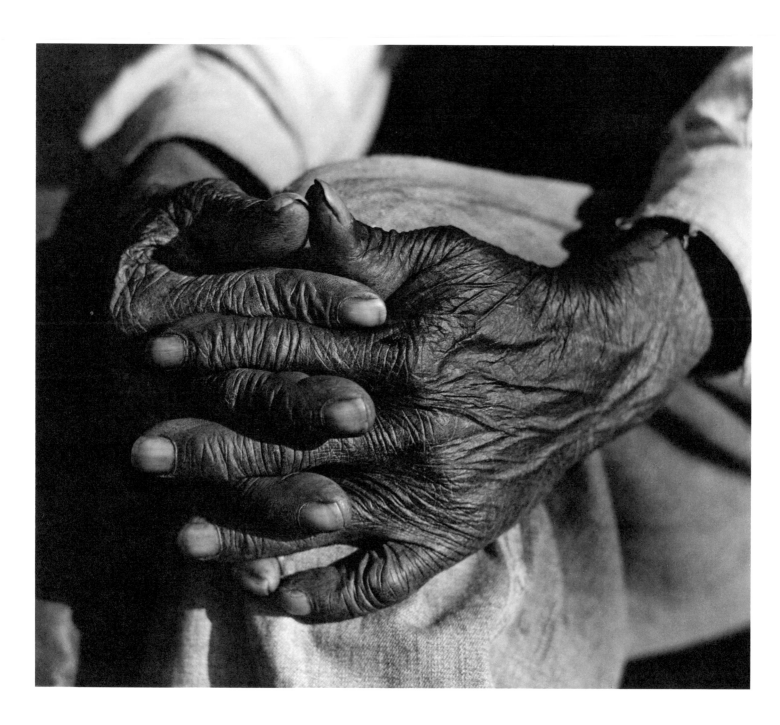

The hands of Henry Brooks, an aged former Georgia
slave, were photographed by Jack Delano in Greene
County in 1941. *Library of Congress*

sat down to write his account of Georgia, there were already 13,000 of them. By the time Georgia was founded, slavery had evolved as a labor system in the United States, and the Englishmen who came to Georgia adopted the caste system already built into American life. La Rochefoucauld, who visited Georgia in 1796, noted that Savannah employed no ships in the slave trade and that bondsmen were carried to Georgia on ships from New England, especially Rhode Island. In 1784 Joseph Clay, a merchant in Savannah, wrote to London: "The Negro business is a great object with us, both with a view to our Interest individually, & the general prosperity of this State & its Commerce. It is to the Trade of the Country, as the Soul to the Body." In 1776 there were 16,000 slaves in Georgia, compared with 15,000 in New York, 80,000 in Maryland, 75,000 in North Carolina and 110,000 in South Carolina. In 1793 Eli Whitney, a young graduate of Yale College who had come to Georgia as a plantation tutor, invented the first commercial cotton gin and transformed the social and economic life of the region. Cotton now replaced the desultory cultivation of rice and indigo on the coast and wheat and tobacco in the interior. In 1800 there were 59,406 slaves in Georgia, 148,656 in 1820, 280,944 in 1840 and 462,198 slaves in 1860. In 1860, of the fifteen slaveholding states, Georgia was second only to Virginia in the number of slaves and slaveowners.

It will never be possible for anyone to present a final and complete portrait of slavery, a complex and always changing institution which has been perceived very differently by succeeding generations of historians. But the memories of bondsmen and travellers, instead of plantation apologists or Northern abolitionists, seem to be the most reliable source. And these indicate that slavery was not an inhuman system, but an intensely human situation, not a perfect order of laws and economics, but a very imperfect accommodation between men who lived together as individuals as well as masters and slaves and

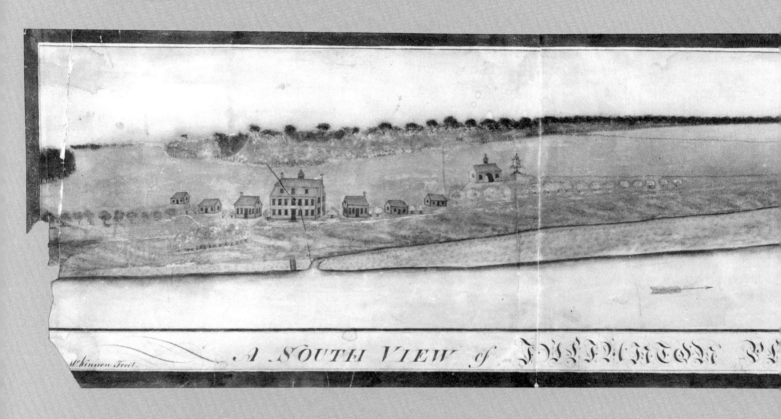

A SOUTH VIEW of PHILIPTON PL

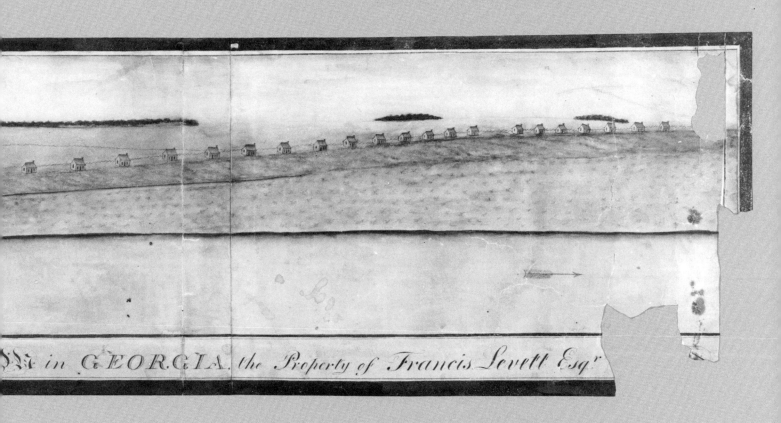

in GEORGIA, the Property of Francis Levett Esq.

Though slavery was outlawed in early Georgia, the institution was legalized in the 1750's and spread rapidly, especially along the coast. The surveyor John McKinney drew this view of Francis Levett's Julianton plantation in McIntosh County about 1796. *Duke University Library*

who had to get along together because they were ultimately dependent on each other. Like most human institutions, slavery had possibilities for benevolence and malevolence. A fugitive slave from Georgia acknowledged: "If there are hard and cruel masters in the South, there are also others of a contrary character. The slave-holders are neither more nor less than men." Fredrika Bremer, a Swedish lady who rode up the Savannah River on a steamer loaded with slaves in 1850, reflected: "There are good and there are bad masters—happy and unhappy slaves." At times, as U. B. Phillips pointed out fifty years ago, slavery may have been harsh and oppressive despotism, resented and resisted; at times it may have been cooperative and affectionate paternalism, received with gratitude and loyalty.

Travellers who came to Georgia before the Civil War recognized that slavery was inconsistent with the professed ideals of American life, but, comparing it with the nasty, brutish and short lives of Europe's laboring poor, they found Georgia's slaves surprisingly content and secure. They acknowledged the moral righteousness of the abolitionists but found unexpected freedom within the slave system. They saw efforts at compulsion and repression, but found the slaves often leading an uncontrollable, underground existence all to themselves. They acknowledged the ties of common experience and even common interests which could bind master and slave together, but found the South suspicious of outsiders and fearful of slaves and freedmen. The travellers viewed immense plantations and hustling cotton centers, but they felt that the condition of the great mass of white people was retarded rather than advanced by slavery.

Immense plantations were not the mainstay of Georgia agriculture before or after the Civil War, despite the moonlight and magnolia mythology which has since obscured the plain realities of southern life. In 1860, there were 2,858 planters, 4,909 overseers, 67,718 farmers

Beverley–House. Country seat of Robert Habersham, Esq.

Near Savannah,

Jan 8. 1844.

Though this drawing of Robert Habersham's "country seat" at Beverley is dated 1844, the house appears to date from the late 18th century. *Private Collection*

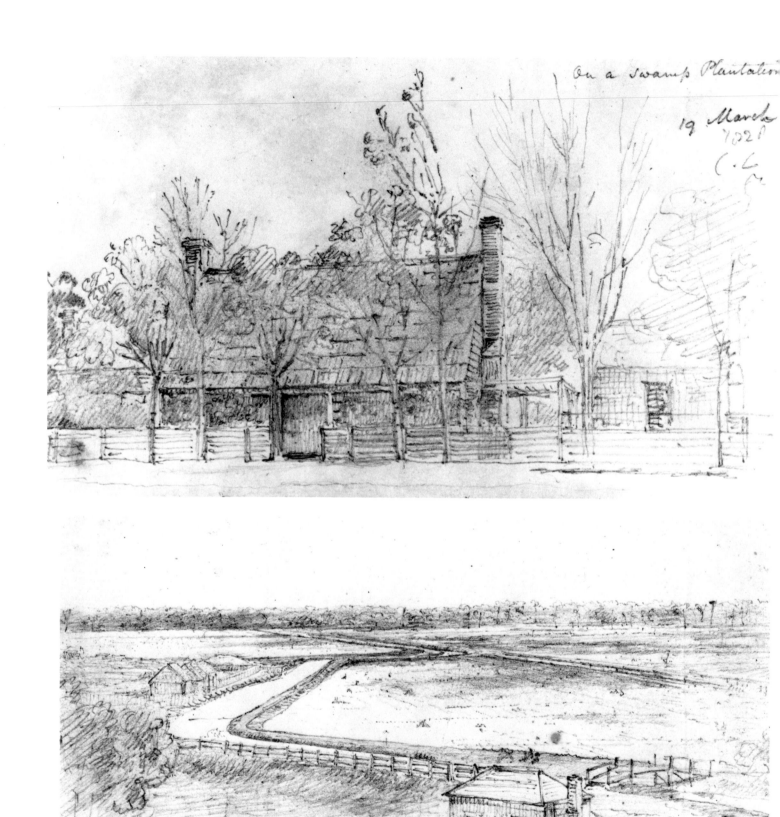

On a swamp Plantation

19 March
1821
(.L.

and 19,567 white farm laborers in Georgia. Of the 53,887 farm-owning families in Georgia in 1860, only 901 cultivated more than 1,000 acres of land with 60–500 slaves, while 2,692 families cultivated 500–1,000 acres with 30–60 slaves, 18,821 families cultivated 100–500 acres with 6–30 slaves, 14,129 families cultivated 50–100 acres with 2–6 slaves, and 13,644 families cultivated 20–50 acres with one slave. The portrait of an average Georgia "planter" which emerges from these statistics is a small proprietor, who works alongside his dozen slaves on his hundred acres of land and shares with them a simple, strong and rather difficult life. Blacks and whites lived in the same backwoods, depended on the same weather and harvests, ate the same cornbread, bacon and molasses, attended the same camp meetings, received the same burials. Letters from planters were preoccupied with three things: the weather, the crops and the health of the slaves. Daily journals of planters record a life of monotonous, unending chores: splitting rails, sowing oats, planting potatoes, cutting sugar cane, spreading manure, chopping the cotton.

The vast majority of Georgia planters lived in modest comfort but without much display or leisure time. Thomas Richardson of Wilkes County died owning four slaves, eleven head of cattle, a dozen hogs, three horses, probably a log house, four pewter dishes, a frying pan, a churn, an iron pot and hooks, one piggin, two axes, a handsaw, a drawing knife and two or three hoes. There were few glass window panes, a paucity of furniture and books. George Womble, a Georgia slave, recalled that there was no real coffee for anyone on the plantation where he grew up. Basil Hall described a plantation house in 1828: "Almost all these forest houses in the interior of the State of Georgia consist of two divisions, separated by a wide, open passage, which extends from the front to the back of the building. They are generally made of logs, covered with a very steep roof. The apartments, at the

The house and rice fields of James Couper's plantation near Darien, drawings by Basil Hall, 1828. *Lilly Library, Indiana University*

end of these dwellings, are entered from the open passage which divides the house in two, the floor of which is raised generally two or three feet from the ground. This opening being generally ten or twelve feet wide, answers in that mild climate the purpose of a veranda, or sitting-room during the day." James Stuart described a similar house in 1830: "The common form of the planters' houses, and indeed of all houses that you meet with on the roadsides in this country, is two square pens, with an open space between them, connected by a roof above and a floor below, so as to form a parallelogram of nearly triple the length of its depth. In the open space the family take their meals during the fine weather. The kitchen and the places for slaves are all separate buildings, as are the stable, corn-houses, etc. About ten buildings of this description make up the establishment of an ordinary planter with half a dozen slaves." Fanny Kemble described her family's house on Butler's Island in 1838: "Three small rooms, and three still smaller, and a kitchen detached from the dwelling—a mere wooden outhouse. Of our three apartments, one is sitting, eating and living room, and is sixteen by fifteen. The walls are plastered indeed, but neither painted nor papered; it is divided from our bedroom by a dingy wooden partition covered all over with hooks, pegs, and nails, to which hats, caps, keys, etc. are suspended in graceful irregularity. The doors open by means of wooden latches, raised by means of small bits of thread. The third room, a chamber with sloping ceiling, immediately over our sittingroom and under roof is appropriated to a nurse and my two babies. Of the closets, one is the overseer's bedroom, the other his office." John Newland spent the night at a planter's house near Macon in 1843: "We were shown into the best room, which was a smooth boarded room, with large crevices in every direction. In one corner was a bed, in another a piano, sofa, marble centre-table, etc., no carpet, and a broken chair put against the door to keep it shut. Our dinner

John MacDonald's house, outside Ringgold in north
Georgia, was built in 1797 and photographed in 1864. It
was a fairly typical Georgia farmhouse. *George Barnard,
Private Collection*

Robert Smith House, Atlanta, c. 1840, is also typical of
Georgia's 19th-century farmhouses. *Van Jones Martin*

consisted principally of bacon and hoe-cake which made me delight-
fully sick." Emily Burke, a New England schoolmarm who came to
Georgia in 1840, described another planter's house: "The house stood
upon four posts about five feet from the ground, allowing a free circu-
lation of air beneath, as well as forming a fine cover for the hounds,
goats, and all the domestic fowls. It was divided into four apartments
below, and two in the roof, and furnished with two broad piazzas,
one in front of the building, where is always the gentleman's sitting
room, and one on the back of the house, where the servants await their
master's orders. The building was slightly covered with boards, arranged like clapboards to shed the rain. This was the entire thickness
of the walls, there being no ceiling, lathing or plastering within. The
floors were all single and laid in so unworkmanlike manner, I could
often see the ground beneath. The roof was covered with log shingles
nailed to the timbers, to save the expense of the boards beneath. Two
chimneys, one upon each end, built of turfs, sticks, blocks of wood,
and occasionally a brick, plastered over with clay, ornamented the
outside of the house." J. T. Trowbridge slept one night at the close of
the Civil War at the home of a planter: "It was a plain, one-and-a-half
story, unpainted, weather-boarded frame dwelling, with a porch in
front and two front windows. The floors were carpetless but swept
clean. The rooms were not done off at all; there was not a lath, nor any
appearance of plastering or white wash about them. The rafters and
shingles of the roof formed the ceiling; the undisguised beams, studs
and clapboards of the frame composed the walls. The dining-room
was a little detached frame box, without a fire-place. There was a
cupboard, a wardrobe, and a bed in the sitting-room; a little bedroom
leading off from it; and two beds in the garret."

Harrison Berry, a Georgia bondsman who published a unique
defense of slavery by a slave in 1861, chastised the self-righteous

abolitionists: "You must recollect, fanatical sirs, that the slave children and their young masters and mistresses are all raised up together. They suck together, play together, go a hunting together, go a fishing together, go in washing together, and in a great many instances, eat together in the cotton-patch, sing, jump, wrestle, box, fight boy fights, and dance together; and every other kind of amusement that is calculated to bolt their hearts together when grown up." Frederick Law Olmsted, the New England landscape architect, creator of Central Park in New York and a professed critic of slavery, recognized these ties of long family association, common tradition, common memories and even common interests which could bind master and slave together. Tyrone Power, the Irish comedian who came to Georgia in 1836, saw the special rapport which could exist among the members of a slaveholding family: "My days were passed at the hospitable home of Mr. G——n, where I was attended by the sleekest, merriest set of negroes imaginable, most of whom had grown old or were born in their master's house; his own good-humoured, active benevolence of spirit was reflected in the faces of his servants." When Sir Charles Lyell, the renowned geologist, visited Hopeton, a coastal Georgia plantation, in 1841, he saw slavery as a benign anachronism in democratic America: "There is an hereditary regard and often attachment on both sides, more like that formerly existing between lords and their retainers in feudal times of Europe, than to anything now to be found in America. The slaves identify with the master, and their sense of their own importance rises with his success in life." John Davis, another traveller, recorded the affectionate greetings received by a Georgia planter when he returned to his family after a trip: "The negroes of the plantation beheld the coming of Mr. Wilson with joy; old and young of both sexes came to the landing place to welcome his approach. The air resounded with exclamations." Fanny Kemble,

Nancy Hart, servant in the family of Tomlinson Fort of Milledgeville. *Georgia Department of Archives and History*

A slave family picking cotton outside Savannah, a photograph of the 1850's by Pierre Havens. *New-York Historical Society*

though uncompromisingly hostile to slavery, reported how gratefully she had been received as the new mistress at Butler's Island in 1838: "No sooner had I disembarked and reached the house, than a dark cloud of black life filled the piazza and swarmed up the steps, and I had to shake hands, like a popular president, 'till my arm ached at the shoulder joint."

Private records reaffirm these published reports of real human relations between masters and slaves. The certificate of freedom for a Georgia slave, dated 1761: "This is to satisfy to whom it may concern that this Black Man, Mr. Moses Handlin is a Free man. . . . This very black Moses Handlin is a very onns Black Man. I knowed him from a Boy." James Habersham wrote to New York in 1764: "Oronoko's wife died last Night, and the poor fellow is inconsolable, and she nursed two of my daughters. I must own the sight of her has affected me more than all the negroes I have ever lost. I have really been obliged to lay down my pen several times." When John Kell of Griffin went off to school at Savannah in 1838, a slave wrote to him: "My dear Master– I hope you are doing well. I know you wont be in bad company though. Your horse is very fat. I always feed him every night & morning. I cried very much the night you went but I hope to see you again my dear master. & be well & hearty. Has your room got a fire place? I hope so, Your boy Ben." When slave Kate's baby died in 1860, her mistress wrote: "My husband and I went out in the morning to select the spot for its burial. We chose a portion of ground and will have it inclosed with a railing. The rain seems to fall on my bare heart." Charles Ball, a fugitive slave, described parting with his dying master: "Tears came in his eyes as he talked to me, and said, that as he could not live long, he hoped I would continue to be faithful to him whilst he did live. This I promised to do, for I really loved my master."

Living was hard work for Georgia's slaves, chopping cotton with backs bent for long hot hours under the naked sun or planting rice

Slaves ploughing fields outside Savannah, a photograph of the 1850's by Pierre Havens. *New-York Historical Society*

with swollen feet immersed for long winter days in cold water. Slaves worked every day of the year, from sunrise to sunset, except Saturday afternoons, Sundays and the week before Christmas and New Year's. They were given assigned tasks each day, which they could complete at their own rate of work, or they were supervised by a driver for a prescribed period of work each day. Houses were small cabins, one for each family. Slaves were provided with one or two suits of clothing for winter and another for summer, one pair of heavy shoes each autumn, a new blanket every two years. Food consisted of pork, corn meal and molasses. Punishments were often severe, and laws delineated a very narrow path for their lives. As personal property, slaves could not own property, make legal contracts or enjoy the rights of citizenship. But laws were often not enforced in the isolated privacy of the Georgia forest. Although the slave codes provided that slaves could not be taught to read, George Womble recalled that on a nearby plantation the owner caught his own son teaching a little slave boy to write. Though Georgia laws gave no legal sanction to slave marriages, the rights of husbands and wives and family life were generally respected, including during slave auctions, when families might be sold only as family groups. A slave could not own firearms, but Charles Ball and William Grimes, two fugitive slaves, were both given old hunting rifles by their masters.

Slaves who were not overtasked could complete their assigned work early in the day and devote some time to pleasure or to raising vegetables or livestock which they could sell for pocket money. Olmsted noted how the slaves were often victimized by "a swarm of Jews" in Southern towns, who sold the simple bondsmen cheap clothing, trinkets or nauseating whiskey diluted with water and tobacco juice. Celestia Avery, a former slave, danced in her cabin at night to the tune of fiddles which she had purchased with money from selling her chickens. In the cities, a slave might be allowed to hire himself out to a

Slaves and their houses on Fort George Island, at th Georgia-Florida border, in the 1850's. *New-York Historical Society*

The best slave houses were made of tabby, a concrete-like mixture of lime, oyster shells, sand and water. Two views of slave quarters on Saint Catherine's Island, photographed about 1870 by J. N. Wilson. *University of Georgia Library*

white man other than his master. This system allowed the slaves to select their own work, keep most of the proceeds of their labor and to be generally responsible for their own lives. When William Grimes's master left Savannah, the slave was left behind to hire himself out; he was able to earn one dollar a day, so, after paying his master three dollars a week, he could keep four dollars for himself. In the woods around plantations and in their own quarters of towns, the blacks seem to have led an uncontrollable, underground life of their own. In 1763 Patrick Mackay complained about the Negroes who wandered to his plantation at night, stealing livestock and vegetables and creating "very great disorder amongst his slaves by debauching his slave wenches." William Grimes could go out and pay twenty-five cents to have his future predicted by a black fortune-teller, a fascinating glimpse of slave life in Southern cities. The existence of patrollers, white men who served as sentries to maintain law and order among the slaves at night, was proof that the blacks were accustomed to doing what they wanted after dark.

Ultimately, however, slaves were always dependent on the disposition of their masters. Cecily Cawthorn, a former slave, recalled: "I had a cousin to run away, and they got her back from Charleston. The overseer gave her a hundred licks. One lick cut the blood, and my mistress got so mad, she quarreled at Marster. He said he had to make an example for the other slaves. Mistis said it injured the woman to whip her that a way, so then Marster made 'em be more careful." An overseer reported how one slave tried to flee in 1861: "George (big) attempted to run off in presents of the entire force and in my presents. He was caught by Driver John. I give him sixty straps in presents of those he ran off in presents of." William Grimes told of begging to escape punishment: "Mr. Sturges was a very kind master, but exceedingly severe when angry. He had a new Negro, by the name of Cato, with whom I got a fighting and bit off his nose, just as my master was

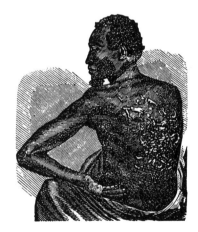

A "badly whipped slave" from Frances Anne Kemble, *The Views of Judge Woodward and Bishop Hopkins on Negro Slavery at the South* (New York, 1863). *University of Georgia Library*

going to sell him, which injured the sale of Cato very much. For this I had to beg very hard to escape being whipped." Leah Garrett, a former slave, recorded: "Everybody always stripped you in them days to whup you, 'cause they didn't care who seed you naked. Some folks' chillun took sticks and jabbed you all while you was bein' beat. Sometimes these chillun would beat you all 'cross your head, and their Ma's and Pa's didn't know what stop was." The regulations on Pierce Butler's plantation set limits to the beating of slaves: field drivers could administer only twelve lashes, the head driver no more than thirty-six, the overseer as many as fifty. Mollie Kensey remembered her slave sister: "They'd make her go out and lay on a table and two or three white men would have intercourse with her before they'd let her up. She was just a small girl." John Brown, a fugitive slave, claimed to be the victim of eccentric medical experiments at the hands of a neighboring planter to test sunstroke remedies by baking him in the sun, to discover the effects of fastings and bleedings, to learn the depth of a Negro's dark skin by blistering and peelings. Georgia laws against "unnecessary and excessive whipping, beating, cutting or wounding, or cruelly and unnecessarily biting or tearing with dogs" were cool evidence that such abuses did exist.

Travellers saw signboards and placards announcing slave auctions and found slave pens surrounded by high walls where the bondsmen were kept for inspection. A typical advertisement might read: "A Cargo consisting of about 170 Young and healthy New Negroes, Chiefly Men, all of whom have had the Smallpox, from Gambia." John Brown, a Georgia slave, was sold by the pound. Moses Roper, another fugitive slave, was put up for auction along with the other valuable property of his late master's estate, including a carriage, horses, a gold watch and cigars. For a time Roper worked for a slave trader in Georgia, and his job was to grease the bodies of the blacks every morning with sweet oil before they were put up for sale, to make

Advertisements for the return of runaway slaves and slave auctions at Savannah, 1787 and 1788, Campbellton, 1846, and Lumpkin, 1859. *Duke University Library (top), Private Collection (bottom)*

24 DOLLARS REWARD.

❖❖❖❖❖❖❖❖❖❖❖❖❖

RAN AWAY from the subscriber, on Friday the 3d instant, about 12 o'clock in the day,

FRIDAY,

A very stout likely Negro Man, about 23 years of age, 5 feet 9 or 10 inches high, marked with *African* marks on his cheeks, and small eyes; he had on when he went away an oznabrig shirt and trowsers, but, as he has a number of other clothes, will probably soon change his dress; he was lately the property of Col. Pannell, of Wilkes county, and it's believed he is now gone to Washington.

S. TUFT.

Savannah, 6th August, 1787.

Run away from the Subscriber,

About eight days ago,

The following Negroes, viz.

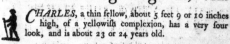

CHARLES, a thin fellow, about 5 feet 9 or 10 inches high, of a yellowish complexion, has a very sour look, and is about 23 or 24 years old.

FRANK, a pretty stout fellow, about 5 feet 8 or 9 inches high, 25 or 26 years old, has had one of his eyes hurt, which is generally weak, has remarkable broad flat feet, a big mouth, and thick lips.

LONDON, about 5 feet 8 or 9 inches high, 23 or 24 years old; is pretty well made, except his feet, which are very broad and flat, had on when he went away a purple negro cloth jacket and trowsers very much worn.

They are all smooth faced, and none of them have any beard, speak good English, and are very artful. *London* can also speak German; he carried off with him a small BROWN BAY MARE, about 12 and an half hands high, 5 years old, with a long switch tail and bushy mane, no brands.

Whoever will deliver the said Negroes to me on Savannah river, or to the Warden of the Workhouse in Savannah, shall receive *a Reward of Three Guineas* each for *Frank* and *London*, and *One* for *Charles.*

GEO. P. READ.

April 2, 1788.

EXECUTOR'S SALES.

AGREEABLY to the last will and testament of Thomas McKoy, Senr. late of Campbell county, deceased, will be sold before the Court House door in the Town of Campbellton, said county, on the first Tuesday in February next,

THE PLANTATION,

Lying on the Chattahoochee River, below and adjoining the Pumpkin Town Fractions, and known as the Foster Place.

ALSO,

The Negroes

Belonging to said estate—consisting of

MEN & WOMEN, BOYS & GIRLS;

Among them are 2 House Carpenters;

and between Thirty and Forty in Number.— *Terms of Sale.*—The Purchaser will be required to pay one half cash, and the balance due on the first day of January, 1848, with good personal security, in sums not exceeding Thirty Dollars. Property sold for a division among the legatees.

JOHN BOWEN, Exec'r.

November 25, 1846.

EXECUTOR'S SALE.

ON the 2nd Monday in January next, will be sold at the residence of Thomas McKoy, senr., late of Campbell county, deceased, all the Perishable Property of said deceased—consisting of *Corn, Fodder & Wheat, Horses, Mules, Cows & Calves, Pork and Stock Hogs,* and other articles not now recollected. Terms made known on the day of sale.

JOHN BOWEN, Exec'r.

Nov. 18, 1846.

Notice To Debtors & Creditors.

ALL Persons indebted to the estate of Thomas McKoy, senr., late of Campbell County, dec'd, are requested to make immediate payment—and those having demands against the estate will present the same, properly attested, for payment, within the time prescribed by law, to

JOHN BOWEN, Exec'r.

Nov. 18, 1846.

NEGROES, NEGROES.

The undersigned has just arrived in Lumpkin from Virginia, with a likely lot of negroes, about 40 in number, embracing every shade and variety. He has seamstresses, chamber maids, field hands, and doubts not that he is able to fill the bill of any who may want to buy. He has sold over two hundred negroes in this section, mostly in this county, and flatters himself that he has so far given satisfaction to his purchasers. Being a regular trader to this market he has nothing to gain by misrepresentation, and will, therefore, warrant every negro sold to come up to the bill, squarely and completely. Give him a call at his Mart.

J. F. MOSES.

Lumpkin, Ga., Nov. 14th, 1859.

them glow with apparent health and vigor. Charles Ball, later a fugitive slave, realized that he would soon be sold from South Carolina into Georgia and reflected: "I was now in a country where the life of a black man was no more regarded than that of an ox, except so far as the man was worth more money in the market." The general rule, in fact, was that an able-bodied field hand was worth $100 for every cent cotton was bringing; thus, a planter figured he could afford to pay $1,000 for a slave when cotton was selling for ten cents a pound. A traveller named Nason in 1848 left work to attend a sale of slaves and horses at Savannah: "Saw fifty-four men, women and children sold as chattels, but not without emotion, to see the serious look, the falling tear, and the submissive will. There are three auctioneers selling at the same time. Sometimes one man is up [for sale], sometimes three or more. Sometimes a woman and children, called 'an interesting family of negroes.' Now a plantation – now, a gun – now, an old man, wife and daughter – now, a young man, etc. etc. The time for this traffic in slaves, and the souls of men, is the first Monday in each month." Former Georgia slaves spoke with affecting simplicity about sales. Willis Cofer: "We used to hear tell of big sales of slaves, when sometimes mammies would be sold away from their chilluns. It was awful, and then they would just cry and pray and beg to be allowed to stay together. At them sales they would put a nigger on the scales and weigh him, and then the bidding would start." George Womble: "I never saw my father as he was sold before I was old enough to recognize him as being my father." Mollie Kensey: "They sold my father in 1858. I never 'member seein' him. See, chile, I was three years old. They sold him from ma and five chilluns." Sally Brown: "I was given away when I was just a baby and I never did see my mama again." Traveller George Lewis met a Georgia slave bound for the New Orleans market

Slave market, Whitehall Street, Atlanta, photographed by George Barnard, 1864.
Library of Congress

OVERLEAF:
A view of Savannah, through Monterey Square and down Bull Street toward the river, by J. Smith, 1856.
Private Collection

who told him: "Master promised I should die in his service. It is mighty bad to sell me. I is heart-break, and I think I will die."

In 1793 Eli Whitney invented the first commercial cotton gin on a plantation near Savannah and transformed the social and economic life of the region. When Whitney came to Georgia, the main crops were rice and indigo on the coast and wheat and tobacco in the interior. Travellers navigating the Savannah River at the time of the Revolution saw only tobacco and corn on the river banks and on the pole barges heading downriver to the sea. In 1773 William Bartram had observed that cotton was planted only by the poorer class of people and then just enough for their family consumption. In 1791 George Washington reported that rice and tobacco were Georgia's most important exports. F. A. Michaux reported at the turn of the century: "The culture of rice has diminished very much within a few years; it has been, in a great degree, replaced by that of cotton, which yields greater profits to the planters." During the next thirty years prices were high and the profits were terrific. Cotton plantations and slaves moved into the lands along the Savannah River and just beyond Augusta by 1800, swept into the rich lands of the central interior by 1820 and proceeded into the newly acquired Indian territory of southwestern Georgia after 1830. Cotton production in Georgia soared from 1,000 bales in 1790 to 90,000 bales in 1820, to 408,481 bales in 1840 and 701,840 bales in 1860.

Now Savannah, a village of sandy, littered streets, was changed by the cotton bonanza into a world port, a real international city to be traded with and reckoned with. Augusta, a frontier fort which had been a depot for the Indian traffic and tobacco trade in the eighteenth century at the falls of the Savannah River, became a busy market for cotton headed downriver to Savannah and the sea. Athens, a hillside village, was established as the new home for the University of Georgia

George Washington Lay and his cousin James Berry Lay, Gordon County, c. 1855. *Georgia Department of Archives and History*

by its governing body, the Senatus Academicus, in 1801. Milledgeville, a raw town at the headwaters of the Oconee River named for Governor John Milledge, was designated the state capital in 1804, only a year after its founding and before even a dozen houses had been built there. In October, 1807, fifteen wagons carried the state's public records from Louisville, the old capital, to Milledgeville. This was a quiet but significant event, which symbolized the shifting of Georgia's population, wealth and power from the coast to the cotton belt. By 1830 two-thirds of the population of Georgia lived within ninety miles of Milledgeville. Macon was laid out in 1823 on the Ocmulgee River near old Fort Hawkins, and Columbus was laid out in 1828 on the Chattahoochee River near old Fort Mitchell. In 1838 Roswell King moved from a coastal plantation to the interior uplands, where he established a cotton factory and a town named in his own honor, Roswell.

Travellers were struck by the passionate preoccupation of the Georgia people with cotton. John Davis dined at Dillon's boarding house, Savannah, about 1800: "There was a large party at supper, composed principally of cotton manufacturers from Manchester, whose conversation operated on me like a dose of opium. Cotton! Cotton! Cotton! Cotton! was their never-ceasing topic. Oh! how many travellers would have devoured up their discourse; for my part, I fell asleep, and nodded till a negro offered to light me to my room." Ebenezer Kellogg sighed at Savannah in 1818: "I hear nothing but talk of the price of cotton. The Georgians are madly devoted to cotton." Adam Hodgson came to Georgia in 1827: "I arrived in Augusta and when I saw the cotton waggons in Broad Street, I whistled! but said nothing. There was more than a dozen tow boats in the river, with more than a thousand bales of cotton on each; and several steam boats with still more. And you must know, that they have cotton warehouses covering whole squares, all full of cotton; and some of the knowing ones told me, that there were then in the place from 40,000 to 50,000

Thomas Jefferson Ruslin of Georgia, 1861.
Library of Congress

bales. It puzzled me to tell which was the largest, the piles of cotton or the houses.'' William Cullen Bryant came to Savannah in 1843: "One should see the multitude of bales of it accumulating in the warehouses and elsewhere, in order to form an idea of the extent to which it is produced in the southern states—long trains of cars heaped with bales, steamer after steamer loaded high with bales coming down the rivers, acres of bales on the wharves, acres of bales at the railway stations.'' John Lamar, a planter from Macon, wrote to Howell Cobb in 1845: "The whole world of planters, buyers, etc. are on tiptoe for the news by the steamer which left Liverpool on the 4th February. My prayers are fervent for advices of a ha'penny advance and large sales, great demand for cotton goods, spinners prosperous, corn plenty and all that sort of parlance, so interesting to us poor toads under a harrow, planters of cotton.'' Fredrika Bremer cruised up the Savannah River in 1850 and saw: "On deck, a few gentlemen, planters, who were polite and wished to talk, but talked only of 'cotton, cotton, cotton.' I fled away from these worshippers of cotton.'' A traveller of 1856 summed up the popular feeling: "A kind of cotton insanity appears to affect all classes. To their distempered imaginations, cotton is the pabulum that nourishes and sustains the rest of mankind; cotton, the 'open sesame' to wealth, honor, and personal and national aggrandizement; cotton, the Atlas which upholds and the lever that moves the entire world.''

People, commerce, steamboats and railroads followed the advance of cotton planting across Georgia. Like fingers stretching from the sea, the Savannah, Altamaha, Oconee and Chattahoochee rivers reached from the coast toward the new plantations. In 1819 a steamboat commenced regular runs between Milledgeville in the interior and Darien on the coast, and soon a fleet of steamers replaced the pole barges which had been carrying cotton from Augusta to Savannah, from Milledgeville to Darien, from Columbus to Appalachicola in

Richard Richardson House, Savannah, 1817–19
Van Jones Martin

Nicholas Ware House, Augusta, 1818.
Van Jones Martin

Florida. In 1826 Wilson Lumpkin surveyed the route for a proposed railroad, to be towed by mules, over the north Georgia mountains. In 1836 construction was commenced on the Georgia Railroad west from Augusta, and in 1837 the Central of Georgia began laying rails from Savannah toward the northwest. Early factories, most of them cotton mills, were established in places like Augusta, Athens, Roswell and Columbus, where water power and cotton plantations came together. Meanwhile, the University of Georgia had been chartered in 1785 and opened in 1801. A Medical Academy was founded at Augusta in 1828. Adiel Sherwood founded Mercer Institute at Penfield in 1831, later supported by the Baptists; Emory College near Covington was established by the Methodists in 1834; Oglethorpe College near Milledgeville was founded by the Presbyterians in 1838.

For the first thirty years after Whitney's invention, the land was cheap, the soil virgin, the slaves prime and the harvest bountiful. But by 1830 the land was becoming dearer, aging slaves a greater burden and abused soil less productive. In the early 1820's and before, a small planter could buy slaves and raise cotton at a substantial profit, but after 1835 he could no longer do so. The cost of land and slaves was rising, while the price of cotton was declining, making it necessary for planters to raise larger and larger crops to survive. Cotton prices ranged from twenty to forty cents per pound in the early nineteenth century and from ten to twelve cents per pound during the 1850's, while the cost of prime field hands rose from $300 in 1790 to $1,600 and $1,800 in 1860. Expressed in terms of cotton, slave prices were soaring from 1,500 pounds of cotton in 1800, to 3,000 in 1810, to 5,000 in 1820, to 7,000 in 1830, to 8,000 in 1840, to 10,000 in 1850 and to 18,000 in 1860. It was symptomatic of the economic stress that planters had to abandon their old practical rule, that they could afford to pay for a field hand a price in hundreds of dollars equal to the price of cotton in cents. Borrowing money to buy more land and more slaves,

James Stirling observed from Macon in 1850, made the indebtedness of Southern planters notorious. John Melish saw indications of this desperate dependence on the price of cotton: "The staple commodity of this state is cotton, and it had so fallen in value, as to cut off upwards of one third of the income. I accordingly found that all the people in the interior of the country were clothed in homespun."

Meanwhile, cotton cultivation was exhausting the farms of Georgia. Many planters had to face an inevitable choice: a few years more, going on at that rate, they must either remove West, be sold out by the sheriff to pay their debts, or live in extreme poverty. Emily Burke wrote in 1840 that Georgia planters had poor houses because they had to move frequently: "One often meets deserted plantations. A plantation is cleared, and a sort of temporary hut erected, then covered with slaves who cultivate the soil as long as it will produce any thing, then left for another to be used in the same way." John Lamar of Macon wrote his cousin Howell Cobb in 1847, giving us a rare insight into the planter's mind: "Lord, Lord, Howell, you and I have been too used to poor land to know what crops people are making in the rich lands of the new counties. I am just getting my eyes open to the golden view. On these good lands, when cotton is down to such a price as would starve us out, they can make money." The new territory was, he said, a veritable promised land. "Buy we must! That is a fixed fact, there is no getting around it. It must be done." As planters tried to buy more land to plant more cotton and weather the economic squeeze, the enlarged plantations pushed out any foundations of a substantial class of independent farmers in Georgia after 1830. In Wilkes County in 1820 there had been 1,057 farmers who owned 8,921 slaves, but by 1857, 469 farmers owned 7,587 slaves, a reflection of the expansion of great plantations and the exclusion of small farmers. James Silk Buckingham recorded this interview in the Georgia cotton belt in 1837: "One of the

Nathan van Boddie House, LaGrange, 1836.
Frances Benjamin Johnston, Library of Congres

Georgia State House, Milledgeville, as remodelled in 1827.
Eberhardt Studio, Milledgeville

farmers, who was upwards of sixty-five years of age, told me that he had made up his mind to migrate next year, to the valley of the Mississippi; and when I asked him what could induce him, now so far advanced in life, and with a large family, to move so far from his home, he replied, that there was too much aristocracy here for him! I asked him who or what constituted the aristocracy of which he spoke. He said they were the rich men of these parts, who bought up all the land at extravagant prices, and left none for the poorer citizens to purchase." By 1850 there were already fifty-nine thousand Georgians in Alabama and seventeen thousand in Mississippi. Cotton land speculators on the western borders of Georgia were said to be swarming thicker than the locusts in Egypt.

By the 1830's, then, people were again on the move across the Georgia frontier, but this time most were leaving rather than entering the state and searching in other places for opportunities which were no longer open for them in Georgia. In 1820 Adam Hodgson observed the first stages of this secondary migration of excluded small farmers and distressed planters from Georgia: "In the course of the day we passed some Indians with their guns and blankets, and several waggons of emigrants from Georgia and Carolina to Alabama. We also saw many gangs of slaves whom their masters were transporting to Alabama and Mississippi, and met one party returning from New Orleans to Georgia. We were astonished to meet this solitary party going against the stream. Often a light carriage, of a sallow planter and his lady, would bring up the rear of a long cavalcade, and indicate the removal of a family of some wealth, who, allured by the rich lands of Alabama, or the sugar plantations on the Mississippi, had bidden adieu to the scenes of their youth and undertaken a long and painful pilgrimage through the wilderness." In 1834 Tyrone Power described other caravans of wagons moving toward Georgia's western border, "each laden, first with the needful provisions and such household gear as may be considered indispensable; next, over this portion of the freight is stowed the family of the emigrant planter, his wife, but commonly a round squad of white-haired children, with their attendants; on the march these vehicles are surrounded by slaves, varying in numbers from half a dozen to fifty or sixty, according to the wealth of the proprietor; a couple of mounted travellers commonly complete the cavalcade, which moves over these roads at the rate of twelve or fifteen miles a day." Power said the numbers of immigrants leaving Georgia for the Southwest were incredible. Georgians had become again nomads passing across an unsettled land.

The economic drain of cotton planting perpetuated an undeveloped agricultural economy. Daniel Turner, a young Rhode Island doctor at Saint Mary's in southernmost Georgia in 1805, wrote his family about the land-poor planters: "I suppose in all Camden County there is scarcely a planter with a hundred dollars by him & perhaps his plantation & Slaves worth a hundred thousand." George Lewis, who travelled through Georgia in 1844, observed: "Nothing was attended to but the rearing of cotton and slaves. The more cotton the more slaves, and the more slaves the more cotton!" This meant that there was little capital used to develop a balanced economy or build a society of shopkeepers, artisans, factories and cities. Charles Lyell in 1846 was struck by the difficulty of raising money in Georgia for building cotton mills: " 'Why,' they say, 'should all our cotton make so long a journey to the north, to be manufactured there, and come back to us at so high a price?' It is because all spare cash is sunk in purchasing negroes." James Stirling wrote: "What capital they save, and that is not much, they lay out in niggers. Niggers and cotton—cotton and niggers; these are the law and prophets to the men of the South." In 1860 forty-six percent of Georgia's wealth was invested in slaves and

Executive Mansion, Milledgeville, 1838–39.
Van Jones Martin

not in the comforts of civilized life or in banks, machinery and ships. Frederick Law Olmsted noted that the cart wheels in Georgia came from the North, that the plows came from New York. According to Charles Lyell, the wife of Georgia's governor did not realize that people outside the South could buy soap in shops instead of always having to make it for themselves at home. James Silk Buckingham proclaimed rhetorically that had Southern capital not been tied up in slaves, it could have been used to advance the region by at least a century.

The undeveloped industrial economy, the region's reputation for slavery and the few opportunities for skilled workers all discouraged the migration of ambitious artisans to Georgia, another element of a cycle of limited growth and diminished opportunity. The work of skilled craftsmanship was done by the slaves, who held a privileged position in the labor market, subsidized, trained and employed by their owners. Charles Lyell visited Columbus in 1846: "Several New Englanders have complained to me that they can not push on their children here as carpenters, cabinet makers, blacksmiths, and other such crafts, because the planters bring up the most intelligent of their slaves to these occupations." In 1855 Frederick Law Olmsted reported: "New England factory girls have been induced to go to Georgia to work in the newly-established cotton factories, by the offer of high wages, but have found their positions so unpleasant—owing to the general degradation of the laboring class—as very soon to be forced to return." A white carpenter at Rome in 1849 complained that the competition of cheap black laborers made it impossible for him to be paid a living wage for his skills. It was reported that some planters hired Irish laborers to do unhealthy work too dangerous for their valuable slave property.

Georgia, like a tender sapling girdled at its trunk, was being strangled by its devotion to cotton and slaves. Town life was eclipsed

arrington Hall, Barrington King House, Roswell, 1840.
an Jones Martin

OVERLEAF:
Oglethorpe University, Milledgeville (tl); Georgia Female College, Macon (bl); Medical College of Georgia, Augusta (tr); and Brownwood Female Institute, LaGrange (br); from W. C. Richard's *Georgia Illustrated* (Penfield, 1842). *University of Georgia Library*

by the predominance of the plantation system. Because of the sparse population, caused by Georgia's considerable territory and the maturing enlargement of plantations after 1830, it would have been difficult for the state to become a cohesive, stable society. Between the Revolution and the Civil War, Georgia's white population increased about eight times, but the land area also increased, by cession from the Indians, about eight times, so the population remained spread out over a large territory. In 1860 the population density in the coast-planting states, an area which included Georgia, was 15.25 persons per mile compared with 50.47 in New England and 69.83 in the Middle Atlantic states. Forty-four percent of those people in the South were slaves, for whom education was forbidden, so it was doubly difficult for Georgia to establish a coordinated system of public education. The original plan for the University of Georgia, product of the idealism of the Revolution, had included a college at Athens and preparatory schools in each county. But the college struggled with difficulty during its early years, when state officials were preoccupied with Indian troubles. At this time the president of the college was its only faculty member, and the college was saved only by selling its land endowment. The system of academies was never built, and no public school system was created until after the Civil War. In 1860, 19.6 percent of all white adult Georgians could not read or write. Between 1802 and 1865 Georgia publishers started more than fifty literary magazines, but most of them, like the famous, fated *Orion*, which was started at Penfield in 1842 and which expired in 1844, were quick failures.

In the eighteenth century, when Habersham and Stokes complained with seaboard snobbery about "crackers," they meant the vigorous men coming into Georgia from North Carolina and Virginia in search of new land. After 1830, when travellers wrote about "crackers," they meant passive poor people living on marginal land deep in

Bulloch Hall, James Bulloch House, Roswell, 1840.
Van Jones Martin

the Georgia forest. In 1860 most white families in Georgia owned no slaves and no land. There were 118,000 white families in Georgia, but only 41,084 families owned slaves, which meant that 75,000 families owned no slaves. With 118,000 white families in Georgia, there were only 53,887 farms, which meant that some 65,000 Georgia families were landless. Notably, these statistics reveal that only some 12,000 farms were cultivated without the use of slave labor, evidence that no class of sturdy, independent farmers had survived the expansion of larger plantations after 1830. It was difficult for these landless families to find work on the land, for the slaves tilled the soil, or to find work in the few cities, where there were few industrial operations and where slaves had become the skilled artisans. Without good land or good jobs in Georgia, those families who were able moved to the West. Some of those who were not able, struggled for subsistence on the poorest land as squatters or renters. So nearly one-half of the white families in Georgia lived a landless, slaveless life in a society based on land and slaves.

Fanny Kemble described the lives of these people in 1838: "Have you visions of well-to-do farmers with comfortable homesteads, decent habits, industrious, intelligent, cheerful and thrifty? Such, however, is not the yeomanry of Georgia. The scattered white population, too poor to possess land or slaves, and having no means of living in the towns, squat on other men's land till ejected. They are hardly protected from the weather by the rude shelters they frame for themselves in the midst of these dreary woods. Their food is chiefly supplied by shooting the wildfowl and venison, and stealing from the cultivated patches of the plantations nearest at hand. Their clothes hang about them in filthy tatters, and the combined squalor and fierceness of their appearance is really frightful." George Featherstonhaugh saw them in the countryside of northern Georgia in 1835: "tall, thin, cadaverous-

Andrew Low House, Savannah, 1850.
Van Jones Martin

153

looking animals, looking as melancholy and lazy as boiled cod-fish." James Silk Buckingham saw them near Macon in 1839: "The appearance of nearly all the men we saw from the country was reckless, dirty, dissipated, and vulgar." Fredrika Bremer saw them in 1850: "One day I went to see, in the forest, some of the poor people, a kind of wretched white people, who live in the woods, without churches, without schools, without hearths, and sometimes, also, without homes." John Brown, a fugitive slave from Georgia, remembered poor whites, too proud or unable to work, who induced the slaves to steal corn and chickens from plantations for them. Charles Ball, another fugitive slave, wrote about the poor whites of Georgia: "There is no order of men in any part of the United States who are in a more debased and humiliated state of moral servitude than are those white people who inhabit that part of the southern country, where the landed property is all, or nearly all, held by the great planters." These people were still leading frontier lives.

Considering the state's slow material and social progress, the handful of rich and accomplished men who built Georgia's cities, railroads, its agricultural, medical, historical and literary societies were truly exceptional men. Thomas Spalding of Sapelo was an inventive genius of truly Jeffersonian dimensions who lived on an island off the coast of Georgia. James Hamilton Couper dispensed urbane hospitality and read from a great private library at Hopeton, his remote property on the Altamaha River in the middle of a tropical swamp. The family of Charles Jones in Liberty County were genteel, cultivated people, with a fluent and literate correspondence, despite their primitive isolation. Crawford Long, a physician who pioneered the use of anesthesia in 1842, did it in a sleepy village of Jefferson, Georgia. William Crawford emerged from the brawling politics of frontier Georgia and nearly became President of the United States. These people,

Dinglewood, Joel Hurt House, Columbus, c. 185
Van Jones Martin

who might take holidays at Madison Springs, Tallulah Falls or Stone Mountain, or Clarkesville in north Georgia, who imported English manners and New York furniture, who sent their sons to Princeton, Yale or, less likely, Harvard, were not a considerable number. Cities like rich Savannah, aristocratic Augusta or bustling Columbus were extraordinary urban developments in a frontier land of forests and widely dispersed plantations.

From the Revolution to the Civil War, Georgia remained a wilderness country, an undeveloped and rather primitive place. People were poor, not from the rigors of pioneer life, but from persistent failure. The land was still undeveloped and unpopulated. James Stirling wrote from Macon in 1857: "Every step one takes, one is struck with the rough look of the whole face of civilization. The country is nowhere well cleared; towns and villages are few and far between, and even those which you see have an unfinished look." William Howard Russell, a London newspaper correspondent, viewed the social landscape from his train as it moved toward Macon during the Civil War: "From the windows of the carriages we could see that the children were barefooted, shoeless, stockingless—that the people who congregate at the wooden huts and grogshops of the stations are rude, unkempt, that the villages are miserable places." The most dramatic signal of Georgia's falling outside the mainstream of American life was that the national frontier had far outdistanced Georgia and crossed the Mississippi. That national frontier, the hopeful threshold of opportunity and confidence that Southern people had glimpsed after the Revolution, had now progressed thousands of miles across the continent, leaving Georgia behind, more and more isolated for another seventy-five years.

William B. Johnston Villa, Macon, 1855.
Van Jones Martin

4. Soldiers and Civilians

By defending his state's interests at the expense of the united Confederate policy, Georgia's Civil War Governor Joseph E. Brown helped undermine the Southern war effort. *University of Georgia Library*

THOUGH Georgia's political leaders had led the Compromise of 1850 in Congress, during the last decade before the Civil War the South's political frustrations had forged a truly regional party and the South's social fears had united white Georgians—people who really had very diverse and conflicting interests—to defend slavery. In 1860 no Republican electors appeared on the ballot in Georgia, and no votes were cast for the Republican candidate. But even before the news reached Georgia, it was recognized that Abraham Lincoln would be elected President. The political frustrations and social fears of a generation now exploded. In November, the state legislature appropriated one million dollars for military purposes, authorized a small army of ten thousand troops and called a convention of the people to decide what response Georgia should make to Lincoln's election. By the time that convention assembled at Milledgeville in January, 1861, four states—South Carolina, Mississippi, Florida and Alabama—had already seceded. The governor, two of the three justices of the State Supreme Court, the two senators and six congressmen from the state and four of the five living former governors favored immediate secession. On January 19, 1861, Georgia became the fifth state to secede from the United States. In February, the state sent delegates to form a provisional regional government at Montgomery in Alabama. Alexander Stephens of Georgia became Vice-President of the new Confederacy, and Robert Toombs of Georgia,

The first flag of Georgia's independence was raised in
Johnson Square, Savannah, in November, 1860. *Lithograph by R. H. Howell, Private Collection*

THUNDERBOLT. BATTERY.

There was little military action in Georgia early in the Civil
War. These soldiers at Thunderbolt Battery outside Savannah
in 1861 idle away their time by fishing, sailing and sunning
themselves. *Drawing by W. D. Grant, Private Collection*

who had expected to become its President, was made Secretary of State. Georgians and Southerners were gripped by thrilling but contradicting emotions of excitement and fear, patriotism and selfishness which they could not perhaps understand.

In January, 1861, a cheerful band of Georgia volunteers sailed down the Savannah River to capture Fort Pulaski, on Cockspur Island at the mouth of the river, before the federal government could fortify it, and their happy, holiday mood demonstrated sadly that they did not foresee the bitter, bloody war ahead of them. William Plane of Baker County expressed the mock-heroic spirit: "'Tis glorious to die for one's country and in defense of innocent girls and women from the fangs of the lecherous Northern hirelings!" Eddie Neufville of Savannah, then a student at Princeton, wrote home: "Won't it be glorious to meet once more in the Republic of Georgia to fight for our Altars and our fires, God and our native land!!! By God that's bully!!! If those infernal Yankees don't get more hot lead than they can digest in a year, then I don't know anything about Southern pluck and shooting!" J. A. Hardee wrote: "I bet, by George, it won't be long before we give the Yankees *hell*!" The South was rushing to secession, confident that a strong show of force would push the other side to compromise and that any war would be brief.

The plain people of the South were also demonstrating that they valued something more than their own lives by, literally, dying to fight. A Georgia volunteer fighting in Virginia, Shephard Pryor, wrote to his wife in July, 1861: "If I fall in this struggle, I feel that I fall in a good cause." K. T. Pound wrote his parents from camp in September: "I tell you, I shall feel like I am fighting for home, sweet home." Benjamin Moody wrote in October: "The sweeter the country will seem to us when we gain our independence. I think when we gain our independence and get back home we will have a jubilee and say truly, 'Our country!' and live a happy people." Shephard Pryor wrote his wife in February, 1862: "As for myself, I expect to live in a noble country, my native South, and [see] her free or die in her

Josh, a slave, went to war with his master. *Georgia Department of Archives and History*

cause. It is for my country, for you and for our children that I enlist to fight in this war." William Stillwell wrote his wife from the front in August, 1863: "I may fall in the next engagement, God only knows. But if I do, I hope I am ready. I feel that I will die in a just cause. If I die, it will be in defense of my country and the liberty of my people." In April, 1861, the Cuthbert Rifles were drilling day and night with eighty-four volunteers—"some very awkward ones," including the local music teacher. Theodore Fogle and other recruits at Tybee Island were as happy and excited as "a pasul of schoolboys on a holiday." Sentiment in favor of secession was strong throughout the state, except in mountainous north Georgia.

After gathering at railheads, Georgia volunteers, armed with an odd assortment of old muskets, hunting rifles and English pistols, and often uniformed in red or blue cloth or local militia outfits (the official gray never became universal because of shortages), carrying sermons against gambling, swearing, drinking and whoring, were ready to go to the Virginia front. Benjamin Mobley confessed to his mother in August, 1861: "Do you think hard of me [for] not telling you good-by? I did not wish to bid you and Sue farewell weeping." All along the route from Georgia to Virginia, excited crowds were waiting to see and cheer the soldiers. In South Carolina, William Batts of Smithville found ladies waiting at the railroad station with large tubs, jars and cans full of buttermilk and teacakes by the baskets full. Ivy Duggan saw demonstrations of affection and patriotism everywhere from Sandersville to Manassas: "Ladies waved their handkerchiefs, bonnets, flowers, secession aprons, flags with both hands. Little boys stand beside the road and [shout], 'Hurrah for Jeff Davis and the Southern Confederacy!'"

B. E. Yerby found the streets of Richmond crowded with people: "When we marched through there, they poked their heads out of the windows and doors and squalled out, 'Hurray for Georgia! Bring me

Volunteer soldiers from Floyd County, c. 1861
Georgia Department of Archives and History

a scalp when you come back!" In Virginia the volunteers were greeted with brass bands, parades in front of pretty girls, inspections by generals dressed in splendid uniforms, inspiring speeches by prominent officials. Soldiers from Georgia could see their leaders at close range. Theodore Fogle described President Davis as "a dried-up specimen of humanity . . . the God of famine." John Wood described Robert E. Lee as "a gray-and bald-headed, wise-looking old man." New horizons were opening to farm boys who had been drawn from routine lives in isolated communities to help make history and create a new nation. Hundreds of miles from home, visiting cities with fancy shops and strange people, rubbing elbows with soldiers from every state in the new Confederacy, watching long trains of wagons and horses wind 'round and through Virginia mountains, surveying horsemen splash into shimmering silver water as they forded a river, with colors flying and gun barrels flashing in the sunlight, Georgia "boys" suddenly realized, perhaps for the first time in all the confusion, that a new Southern nation was being born.

The people of Georgia embraced secession hastily and without preparation, because they did not expect any war. Georgia simply lacked the population, capital and experience of manufacturing industry necessary to wage a war. During the 1820's the state legislature had laid out inland towns at the headwaters of the major rivers, the most interior places where ships from the coast could navigate. The first steamers did not travel to Macon until 1829 and regular service did not commence until the early 1830's. The new cities, Columbus and Macon, with older Augusta, were centers for local cotton markets. They became manufacturing towns only incidentally, putting to good use the water power and cotton supplies close at hand. The major railroads in Georgia were chartered in the 1830's, their main routes completed in the 1840's and short routes added in the 1850's. But these railroads merely replaced the steamboats, which had replaced the pole

Harrison Nations of Whitfield County bristled with the weapons of war—a rifle, bayonet, a pistol and a knife.
Georgia Department of Archives and History

barges, serving the needs of agriculture and not diversified commerce. The rapid economic expansion of Georgia during the 1850's was limited to grain milling, lumbering and cotton manufacturing.

Three generations of Georgians had invested almost everything in land, slaves and cotton. Georgia was the largest state east of the Mississippi, but its population was small and sparsely settled. Agriculture had meant a static economic tradition. The undeveloped industrial economy, the region's reputation for slavery and the few job opportunities all discouraged the migration of skilled artisans and workers to Georgia, another element of a cycle of limited growth and opportunity. The cheapness of labor made inventiveness and machinery unnecessary. In 1860 there were only four cities in Georgia with more than 5,000 people, and only 4.9 percent of the people of Georgia lived in them. Only 11,575, or 1.9 percent of Georgians worked at manufacturing jobs. In 1860, only $10,890,975 was invested in industry, while $202,694,855 was invested in slaves. At the war's outbreak there was no heavy industry in Georgia, except three foundries in Macon which made railroad supplies, so the state found herself engaged in a war without the means to wage it. Governor Brown appealed to the people to turn in their hunting guns for the state's defense. The difficulty of securing firearms became so great that the governor raised a battalion of troops armed only with wooden pikes. Because they were so poorly equipped, many of Georgia's first recruits were not accepted by the Confederate government. At Savannah, Josiah Tattnall took command of a "mosquito fleet" of four ships —an old paddle-wheeled passenger steamer and three remodelled tugboats—Georgia's entire "navy" in 1861 and a further reflection of the state's economic situation.

The self-imposed isolation of secession compelled Georgia to become more self-sufficient. All kinds of miscellaneous products which

Fort McAllister, on the Ogeechee River outside Savannah, 1864.
Library of Congress

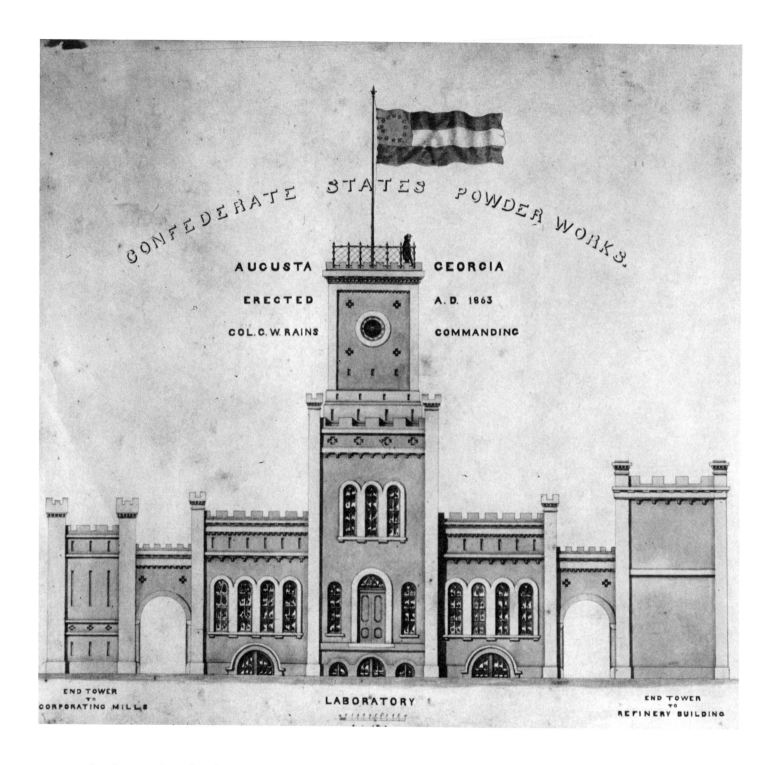

CONFEDERATE STATES POWDER WORKS

AUGUSTA   GEORGIA

ERECTED   A.D. 1863

COL. C. W. RAINS   COMMANDING

END TOWER
TO
CORPORATING MILLS

LABORATORY

END TOWER
TO
REFINERY BUILDING

Georgia, an agrarian and rural state, hastened to industrialize. The Confederate States Powder Works was built at Augusta. *Private Collection*

had been imported—like furniture, coffins, matches, ink and paper, glass, medicines and farm machinery—now had to be produced within the state. The tremendous public spending of the war stimulated Georgia's economic development. Mechanics and factory workers were exempt from the Confederate draft. The state government established a powder mill and gunshop at Augusta, a cannon factory at Rome, others at Athens, Milledgeville, Columbus and Macon. In 1861 the legislature offered ten thousand dollars to anyone who would build a cannon factory. Arsenals were set up in Atlanta, Savannah, Macon, Augusta and Columbus, and the state penitentiary at Milledgeville was converted into a rifle factory in 1862. Confederate quartermasters built garment shops at Augusta, Atlanta and Columbus. There was not only more economic development during the war but also a different quality of growth. Significantly, while no new cotton mills were opened in Georgia, eight new iron mining companies were chartered during 1861–63. True industrial products were made in Georgia for the first time. Factories which had made only the simplest railroad supplies before 1861 now produced other machinery and equipment. Atlanta's rolling mill, no longer just reworking railroad iron, began making heavy plate for gunboats. The Athens Foundry became a cannon factory. The static inertia of agrarian life close to the land was disrupted by the war, as people moved to the cities and turned to factory work. Georgia society became more specialized with professionals, producers and consumers. The Civil War, the first "modern war," brought the industrial revolution to Georgia.

The war stimulated production of farm products across the Georgia countryside, and wartime restrictions on cotton planting prodded reluctant farmers to diversify their crops. From the mountains to the coast, Georgia became a vast harvest land of corn, wheat, sugar, lumber, rice and livestock. The well-filled corn, wheat and oat cribs which Sherman's army found proved Georgia's agricultural productivity, even while distant Virginia was suffering. Fenwick Hedley, who marched with Sherman, called Georgia "literally a land overflowing with milk and honey." Nineteen-year-old Jezze Dozer of Illinois wrote from Big Shanty, Georgia: "I went and got some apples and kooked them for supper. The wheat is getting nearly ripe. Corn knee high. Our teemsters are reeping the wheat and feeding it to their teems. The Citizens here think the yankees are harvesting their wheat too soon." Dolly Lunt Burge faced the bluecoat invasion at Covington: "Like demons they rush in! To my smoke-house, my dairy, pantry, kitchen, and cellar, like famished wolves they come, breaking locks and whatever is in their way. The thousand pounds of meat in my smoke-house is gone in a twinkling, my flour, my meat, my lard, butter, eggs, pickles, wine are all gone. My eighteen fat turkies, my hens, chickens, and fowls, my young pigs are shot down in my yard." John Van Duser, a Union officer, recorded: "I have never seen a country better supplied than this—Turkeys Chickens Geese beef Cattle Sheep & swine in abundance. The story of starvation in the South is played out." From Savannah George Hanger wrote his family in Ohio: "Does every body talk of starving out the rebel army? If so, I think that if they had of been on this trip it would make converts of them. Of all the sweet potatoes and molasses that I ever saw, this state beats them all."

The future site of Atlanta had been uninhabited Indian territory until 1821, but the economic impact of the war transformed the place into a boom town with the prospect of future greatness. During the early 1840's three converging railroads—the Western and Atlantic to Chattanooga and the Midwest, the Georgia Railroad to Augusta and South Carolina, the Macon and Western Railroad south toward the coast—came together at a village first called "Terminus." Before the W&A was built and attention was riveted on the new town of Atlanta,

Fort Pulaski, built by the Federal government on Cockspur
Island near Savannah over a prolonged period 1828–47,
was ocupied by Georgia volunteers in January, 1861. *Fort
Pulaski National Monument*

The Federal fleet had come to the Southern coast in late
1861, and their gunboats began roaming up the Savannah
River and, here, the Ogeechee River, where the Union
ironclad *Montauk* attacked the Confederate steamship
Nashville in February, 1863. *Lithograph by Currier and
Ives, Museum of the City of New York*

most people in Georgia expected Macon, at the center of the state, to become the state's great city and next capital. Robert Somers, who came to Atlanta in 1870, caught the spirit of Atlanta's birth: "The various railroads which meet at this crowded point do not go to the town; the town is gathering in thick and hot haste about the railways." One local citizen boasted, "I guess the railways were here before the people came to Atlanta . . . the new city rising up around the place where it was convenient for the locomotives to be fed with wood and water." In 1847 Atlanta was still a shanty town of twenty-five hundred inhabitants, thirty stores, two hotels, surrounded by woods, the streets filled with stumps but alive with people and progress. There were no churches then and preaching was held, prophetically, in the railroad depot. Charles Olmstead remembered Atlanta in the 1850's as "a sorry-looking place, always associated in my mind with rain and a super abundance of red-clay mud." Felix DeFontaine, war correspondent of the Charleston *Courier*, complained in March, 1862, that Atlanta's sea of mud was "six inches deep and rising." Pedestrians were cautioned to cross streets only on stepping-stones which rose above the mire, and gentlemen were obliged to tuck their trousers into their boots. In 1861, Atlanta's promoters made a determined, though unsuccessful, effort to make their city the capital of the new Confederacy. There were so many strangers coming to Atlanta during the busy war years that street signs had to be put up for the first time. Atlanta's population increased from 11,468 in 1860 to more than 16,000 before the war's end. In a new era of interstate commerce inaugurated by the Civil War, Atlanta would become the great regional distribution center of the South. Significantly, railroad mileage in Georgia increased thirty percent during the decade of the Civil War, despite the considerable destruction at the close of that struggle. Sherman's burning of Atlanta in 1864 was the most dramatic possible recognition of the city's growing importance.

There was no sustained military action in Georgia until Sherman entered the state in May, 1864, though the war had raged in Virginia, Tennessee and Mississippi for three cruel, destructive years. The uncooperative, independent policies of Georgia's Governor Joseph E. Brown were, for the Confederate government at Richmond, nagging and insulting evidence of Georgia's wartime isolation and prosperity: Brown interfered with Confederate conscription agents trying to raise troops in Georgia, he withdrew Georgia troops from Confederate service, he forbade the transportation of firearms beyond state lines, he insisted on naming the officers in Georgia's units of the Confederate Army, he exempted large numbers of persons from Confederate military service so he could keep them within Georgia to defend his own state, he instigated abortive peace negotiations with General Sherman near the end of the war, he led a fierce personal attack on Jefferson Davis.

In October, 1861, a fleet of forty-one federal ships had sailed to Port Royal in South Carolina and, after forcing the Confederates to a hasty retreat, the invaders landed just twenty-five miles from Savannah. By December the Federal forces had surrounded the mouth of the Savannah River and enemy gunboats began cruising around the coastal islands of Georgia. In April, 1862, Fort Pulaski was captured, sealing the blockade of the port of Savannah. But the Federals never tried to attack the city from the sea. There were minor military episodes along the coast. In April, 1862, Federals and Confederates tangled at Whitemarsh Island; in March, 1863, Northern troops tried without success to dislodge the Confederates at Fort McAllister, an earthenwork fortification on the Ogeechee River outside Savannah; in June, 1863, the Federals destroyed a bridge over the Turtle River near Brunswick; and in July, 1863, the coastal town of Darien was burned. In north Georgia there were two attempts to cut the Western and Atlantic Railroad. In

In April, 1863, after surrounding the garrison, the Federal forces bombarded Fort Pulaski. Modern rifled cannon rippe open the walls of the supposedly impregnable brick fortifica tion. *Library of Congress*

April, 1862, Captain James Andrews led twenty soldiers disguised as civilians in the daring theft of a train parked outside Marietta. The raiders fled toward Tennessee, destroying bridges and tracks behind them, until their engine ran out of fuel and they were captured. In April, 1863, Abel D. Streight and his cavalry of sixteen hundred men were repulsed near Rome and captured just across the Alabama line by Nathan Bedford Forrest. In September, 1863, a terrible battle was fought at Chickamauga Creek, but it was part of the Tennessee campaign around Chattanooga and took place only incidentally in Georgia. In the early spring of 1865, months after Sherman had left Georgia and a week after Lee's surrender, General James M. Wilson made a cavalry raid from Columbus to Macon.

But the people of Georgia did join in the war and suffer, if from a distance. About 125,000 Georgians fought in the Civil War, and about 25,000 of them were killed. In 1870 there would be 10,000 *fewer* young white men in Georgia, twenty to twenty-nine years of age, than there had been in 1860. Richard Malcolm Johnston wrote to Alexander Stephens in 1861: "It is a sad sight to see our young men go away to war, and to hear the lamentations of mothers, wives and sisters. I have seen three companies go away already." A Butts County wife, named Mollie Evans, wrote her husband in 1863: "I am very lonesom evry Sunday since you left. I am lonesom all the time but I am worse evry Sunday. I wish you was her to go to meeting with me to morrow and next day. I had rather you were home and I and you living in A doll house then to live in the finest house in the state with out you present. I think of you often in the day and my last words at night is A prayer in behalf of you." William Fisher of Baker County wrote his wife in June and July, 1862, from Virginia: "I cannot describe the battle field. I would to God it could be the last & our country saved. . . . The dead lying all around, your foes unburied. The stiffened bodies lie, grasping

Top: More than two thousand slaves were conscripted from nearby plantations to build emergency fortifications around Savannah in 1863. Bottom: Hundreds of slaves straggled behind Sherman's army as it marched across Georgia in 1864. Woodcuts from pictorial newspapers. *New York Public Library (top), Private Collection (bottom)*

in death the arms they bravely bore, with glazed eyes and features blackened by rapid decay. The air is putrid with decaying bodies of men & horses. My god, My God, what a scourge is war."

Angus McDermid, a farmer's son from Adel, Georgia, entered the army in 1861, with the girls waving handkerchiefs as he marched in parade. At training camp he tasted barracks life: "We are all hear in a house some fiddling and some playing cards and some cussing. . . . Cussing I never did hear the like in all my life." In November, 1861, he heard the mutter of federal cannon at Sapelo Island and shuddered: "I am willing to dy on the battle field if it is my lot. A many a por fellow died on the battle field las Thursday but it is an honerable death to them." Hospitalized in July, 1862: "Now I will tell you what a sick man gets to eat hear. They get one cracker and a cup of coffee and a sick man cant eat that for I cant when I am well. You may no that we fair like dogs hear." The war brought Angus maturity, April, 1863: "Oh father, your letter how sad I felt after I red it. I could not read it without crying for it put me in remembrance of what a bad boy I hav bin in my life and is yet but I have quit a heepe of my wayes and is more sturdy than I was." In July, 1863, there was a bombardment: "I was in five foot of Major Lain when he was killed. His whole head was shot off. His brains flew all over several of us. I never got hit with any ball but a miner ball went through my hair and Mother let me tell you I was hid behind a house one time when the shells was a falling thicker than hail." After the battle of Chickamauga Angus was homesick, September, 1863: "I never did want to go home so bad in all my life as I do now. I think while I was at home I thought that it was a bad place, but I was a fool for thinking so. Home is the best place in this world that I ever hav seen." In November, 1863: "I was glad to get the sox but I cant ware them til I get shoes." In March, 1864, desertions increased: "The Jeneral . . . had a man Branded yesterday on the left hip with a letter D

Union soldiers pose proudly with the cannons in capture Fort Pulaski, 1863. *New-York Historical Society*

Over 13,000 Union prisoners died at Andersonville Prison, outside Macon. *Lithograph by John Walker, Library of Congress*

for deserting." Near Marietta, June, 1864: "I am so black and dirty the clothes that I hav got on me I hav had on 7 weeks. I haint got no cloths only what is on me." After the battles for Atlanta in September, 1864: "I went over the Battle ground since the fite. I tell you the men is their thick and a little dirt put on them. It smells awful shore. I cant stand hardly to smell a dead man and dead horses." Marching in October, 1864, northwest of Atlanta: "In these 3 days march we have lost some where a bout 6000 our men deserted. . . . Mother I am a heep harder hearted than I ought to be but I hav seen so many men killed and wounded till I dont care for it no more than if it was a chicken." Angus died in December, 1864, fighting in Alabama.

By the end of 1864, the Civil War was rushing to a conclusion and the Confederacy was fast disintegrating. During the autumn, General William T. Sherman with sixty-two thousand men, thirty-five thousand horses, mules and cattle, twenty-five hundred wagons, six hundred ambulances and a horde of stragglers marched across the heart of Georgia. His purpose was to destroy the enemy's economic system and to demoralize the civilians. Already Union forces held the Mississippi River and territory north of Vicksburg and St. Louis in the West and everything north of the Tennessee River and most of Tennessee and Virginia in the East. All the Confederate seaports had been blockaded and outside Atlanta Sherman heard first news that Farragut had entered Mobile Bay. While Sherman was penetrating into Georgia, Grant was advancing on Richmond. In the North, Sherman's triumphant procession through Georgia in the bosom of the South strengthened the war party at a critical time and insured President Lincoln's reelection in November. In the South, the march brought an apocalyptic revelation that the war had been lost.

In May, 1864, General Sherman's army left Tennessee and crossed into Georgia. Chauncey Cook, a seventeen-year-old soldier from Wis-

General William T. Sherman, c. 1865.
Library of Congress

consin, wrote from north Georgia, explaining the situation to his parents: "If we can take Atlanta, now the strongest fortified city in the South, we can march to the sea, and then [say] good-bye to the rebellion." The march would follow the Western and Atlantic Railroad from Chattanooga to Atlanta, the Macon and Western Railroad from Atlanta toward Macon and the Central Railroad to Savannah. In the north Georgia mountains, the Union army of ninety-nine thousand faced an inferior Confederate force of forty-four thousand. The Confederate commander, Joseph E. Johnston, tried to avoid direct tests of strength, carefully choosing well-defended ground, fading and dodging back behind destroyed bridges and railroads, while Sherman's greater force was able to outflank the rebels and push them back relentlessly toward Atlanta. On June 27 Sherman launched a costly and unsuccessful direct assault on Kennesaw Mountain, which was held by the Confederates, but by again outflanking them he forced Johnston's men into Atlanta's trenches, the final retreat. On July 17, Johnston was relieved of command by President Jefferson Davis. The new commander, John B. Hood, attempted to regain the initiative with two disastrous, impulsive offensives at Peachtree Creek and Ezra Church during the last days of July. After Sherman had bombarded Atlanta for forty days, part of the federal force swung around south of the city, threatening the Confederate supply routes leading to Macon. When Hood found he could not check this Union force at Jonesboro, he was compelled to evacuate Atlanta on September 1.

These mountain campaigns brought the terrible horror of the Civil War home to Georgia. The soldiers faced wild, desperate dashes across picket lines, under screaming artillery shells and shrapnel, struggling through obstructions, tripping, falling, rising to fall again, rushing on toward more intense gunfire and the probability of death. Theodore Upson, a nineteen-year-old Indiana volunteer, recorded the action in mid-August: "Yesterday the Johnnies attacked us with a

On June 27, 1864, General Sherman launched a costly
and unsuccessful assault on Kennesaw Mountain, but by
flanking the Confederates he forced them to make a final
retreat into Atlanta. *Drawing by William Waud, Library
of Congress*

The Confederate lines outside Atlanta, 1864.
George Barnard, Library of Congress

heavy force. They charged our works. We could see them plainly. Orders were given to hold our fire till they got close. When we did open up their lines seemed to melt away. Time after time those brave desperate men tried to advance their line, but it was of no use." The troops, many of them boys, were offered liquor to stiffen their courage before battle. Union veterans remembered how the Confederates, like men who knew they were throwing away their lives, would charge with their hats pulled down low over their eyes, so they could not see the certain destruction awaiting them. At Dalton in April, Benjamin Smith of Illinois found unburied Union dead, lying naked in the hot blistering sun, stripped of clothing by the retreating rebels. Near Marietta, Sherman wrote his wife at the end of that brutal summer: "It is enough to make the whole world start at the awful amount of death and destruction that now stalks abroad. I begin to regard the death and mangling of a couple of thousand men as a small affair, a kind of morning dash—and it may be well that we become so hardened." From May to September, 4,988 Union soldiers and 3,044 Confederates were killed in Georgia. In July and August, 62,750 northern and 46,332 southern soldiers were hospitalized—one in every two Confederates and one in every three Federals each month. Malaria, typhoid fever, diarrhea, dysentery, exposure, measles, chicken pox did the work which battle wounds could not accomplish.

As Sherman's army advanced, the Georgians fell back in dismay. From Marietta, Sherman wrote his wife: "We have devoured the land. All the people retire before us and desolation is behind. To realize what war is one should follow our tracks." In Marietta there was confusion and panic, the Sisters of Charity loading hospital bedsteads and mattresses into wagons, slaves staggering under burdens of hastily assembled belongings and locomotives steaming up and down the tracks. Minerva McClatchey, who chose to remain at Marietta while her husband fled to south Georgia, saw alarmed citizens with slaves,

A panoramic view of Atlanta, seen from the top of the
Female Seminary, showing the area from the Medical
College on the left to Peachtree Street on the right, in
October, 1864. *Library of Congress*

horses, cows, hogs and sheep racing ahead of Sherman, heard picket guns and skirmishing in the surrounding woods, with the shrieks and cries of wounded soldiers who passed on ambulances, and finally faced an invasion of rough, strange men. The roads into Atlanta were lined with carcasses of horses, hogs and cattle, and the air was heavy with the stench of death and gunpowder. As Sherman's triumphant army passed, the sallow, defeated poor whites watched from the sides of the roads. When Chauncey Cook of Wisconsin tried to offer people Confederate money, they merely smiled sadly and shook their heads. James Patton, an Indiana doctor who had joined Sherman at Chattanooga, saw a young woman on the roadside before Atlanta, skinning a dead cow, while her starving little girl tore at the raw, bloody meat with both hands. Jezze Dozer, that Illinois boy, wrote from outside Atlanta in July: "I could see a sad heart in every man's face."

As refugees and soldiers began to fall back into beleaguered Atlanta, emergency hospitals were set up in the streets. Kate Cumming, a Confederate nurse, found herself surrounded by hundreds of dirty, bleeding and weary soldiers. At times physicians had only old tent cloth to bandage wounds, and the soldiers were eating with their fingers because there were no dishes, knives or forks. Rufus Mead of Connecticut described such a frantic hospital scene on the Union side after the battles for Atlanta: "The poor fellows lay there wounded in every part of the body, some crazy & raving and others suffering all that mortals can. Doctors were busy cutting off limbs which were piled up in heaps to be carried off and buried, while the stench even then was horrible. Flies were flying around in swarms and maggots were crawling in wounds before the Drs could get time to dress them." In Atlanta, ten-year-old Carrie Berry huddled in her basement, while exploding shells fell in the garden outside. As trainloads of wounded soldiers fled Atlanta, the Female College and most of the churches in

Federal pickets outside Atlanta, 1864.
George Barnard, Library of Congress

The ruins of central Atlanta, 1864.
George Barnard, Library of Congress

Macon were turned into hospitals, and when there was no more shelter in Macon, more hospitals were established at Milledgeville. When Macon was evacuated a few weeks later, Eliza Andrews would see houses boarded up, ragged foot soldiers ready to march but not knowing where, fearful civil officials emptying liquor into the gutters.

General Hood abandoned Atlanta on September 1, after destroying eighty-one carloads of ammunition. Outside the city, Sherman's soldiers could hear the blasts and see the red glow of fire from these explosions. In a few weeks the city's population had dropped from more than sixteen thousand to less than three thousand. General W. P. Howard reported to Governor Brown how he had discovered two hundred and fifty wagons of deserters, stragglers and country people plundering Atlanta during that quiet interlude, like the eye of a hurricane, between the Confederate retreat and the federal advance. Sherman's army found the houses perforated with shells and trees splintered with cannon balls. Sherman ordered the civilians to leave the city, offering them transportation to the North or to a neutral camp, called Rough-and-Ready, if they were determined to flee farther south. On November 15, as his army was preparing to leave the city, Sherman ordered his chief engineer to destroy by powder and fire the depot, storehouses and machine shops of Atlanta. Buildings which would not burn were demolished with battering rams. Drunken soldiers, flanked on both sides by burning buildings, raced up and down the streets on foot or horseback. Sherman's aide George Nichols recorded the scene: "The heaven is one expanse of lurid fire; the air is filled with flying, burning cinders; buildings covering two hundred acres are in ruins or in flames; every instant there is the sharp detonation or smothered burning sound of exploding shells and powder concealed in the buildings, and then the sparks and flame shoot away up into the black and red roof, scattering the cinders far and wide." Henry Hitchcock, Sherman's adjutant, saw "the grandest and most awful scene . . . immense and raging fires, lighting up the whole heavens. First bursts of smoke, dense, black volumes, then tongues of flame, then huge waves of fire roll into the sky; presently the skeletons of great warehouses stand out in relief against and amidst the sheets of roaring, blazing, furious flames. Now and then there are heavy explosions; it is a line of fire and smoke, lurid, angry, dreadful to look upon." Most of the central part of the city, but not all of Atlanta, was burned. James Patton glanced back toward the city as the federal army departed on November 15, and, in the brilliant glow of the flaming ruins: "We could see Atlanta burning. I looked at my watch and could see the time very plainly at a distance of ten miles."

Sherman abandoned his supply lines in Tennessee, cut the telegraph wires and moved boldly into the interior of Georgia. For nearly a month the people of the North knew what his army was doing only from reports in Confederate newspapers. From Atlanta the Union army marched in three parallel columns, five to fifteen miles apart, forming a thirty- to sixty-mile front, making good ten to fifteen miles each day across country. The right wing, commanded by Major-General Oliver Howard, moved through Jonesboro, Monticello, Gordon, Irwinton. The left wing under Major-General H. W. Slocum headed to Covington, Madison, Eatonton, Milledgeville. Brigadier-General Judson Kilpatrick led cavalry which struck toward Macon, fell back to Gordon and rejoined Sherman at Milledgeville. The governor and legislature, then in session, hastily abandoned the state capital. The governor pardoned all prisoners in the penitentiary who would join the militia. Sherman's army entered Milledgeville on November 22, burning the depot, arsenal and penitentiary and blowing up the magazine, but not destroying the capitol itself or the governor's mansion. Federal soldiers held a mock session of the legislature and repealed the secession ordinance. The army marched to Sandersville, Louisville and Millen, where the railroad depot was burned on

On December 13, 1864, the Federal forces captured Fort McAllister, the last impediment to Sherman's entry into Savannah. *A. S. Cooley, Library of Congress*

Sherman entered Savannah in late December, 1864, and
reviewed his triumphant troops in front of the U.S. Custom House on Bay Street. *Drawing by William Waud,
Library of Congress*

December 3. On December 13, federal forces under General W. B. Hazen attacked and captured Fort McAllister, a simple earthenwork fortification on the Ogeechee River which separated Sherman's army from the federal fleet off the Georgia coast. During the dark night of December 20, the Confederates abandoned Savannah, retreating silently across the river on pontoon bridges which had been strewn with rice straw to muffle the sound of horses and wagons. Early the next morning the citizens of Savannah surrendered their city without vain resistance, and Sherman dispatched his famous wire to President Lincoln: "I beg to present to you as a Christmas gift the city of Savannah, with one hundred and fifty heavy guns and plenty of ammunition, also about twenty-five thousand bales of cotton."

For the federal army, the march through Georgia was, as one soldier described it, "one big picnic." Sherman's men had tramped from Atlanta to the sea without opposition. There had been only women and children, most of them hiding. There had been plenty of food, the war seemed to be ending and the mood of the victorious army was jubilant. George Bradley, a Wisconsin chaplain, wrote from the outskirts of Milledgeville in late November: "The soldiers seem cheerful and happy, and all, or nearly all, are pleased to have a part in this, the *grandest affair* of the whole war. I heard one say, a day or two since, that he would not have missed it for fifty dollars." George Sharland, an Illinois private, saw his comrades burden themselves with reckless bounty, unskinned pork meat speared on the points of their bayonets, meal and flour filling their haversacks, and frying pans, coffee pots and kettles tied to their knapsacks. Rufus Mead of Connecticut summed up the march from Savannah in December: "We had a glorious old tramp right through the heart of the state, rioted and feasted on the country, destroyed all the RR, in short found a rich and overflowing country filled with cattle hogs sheep & fowls, corn sweet potatoes & syrup, but left a barren waste for miles on either side of the

Two views of the eerily still and silent river-front at Savannah, after Sherman's capture of the port in December, 1864, seen from the steeple of the City Exchange.
Library of Congress

road, burnt millions of dollars worth of property, wasted & destroyed all the eatables we couldn't carry off and brought the war to the doors of the Georgians so effectively, I guess they will long remember the Yankees. I enjoyed it all the time we had pleasant weather & good roads, & easy times generally."

The march brought disaster and the profound sorrow of defeat to the people of Georgia. Civilians saw their own troops steal and plunder. Confederate deserters and stragglers preceded and followed Sherman's army. The newspapers of Georgia and Confederate leaders called upon the people to destroy their supplies and stock to keep the invaders from getting them. Sherman estimated the destruction in Georgia at $100,000,000, of which $80,000,000 was mere waste. General Howard estimated that his wing of the army had burned 3,523 bales of cotton, carried off 9,000 head of cattle, 931 horses and 1,850 mules, consumed or destroyed 9,000,000 pounds of corn and fodder, taken up 191 miles of railroad. General Slocum estimated his wing of the army had captured or consumed 919,000 rations of bread, 1,217,527 rations of meat, 483,000 rations of coffee, 581,534 rations of sugar, 1,146,500 rations of soap, 137,000 rations of salt, 4,090 horses and mules, 11,000,000 pounds of grain and fodder, 119 miles of railroad, 17,000 bales of cotton. General Kilpatrick added 14,000 bales of cotton, 12,900 bushels of corn and 160,000 pounds of fodder. Mary Jones and her pregnant daughter faced invading bluecoats in Liberty County for a month, at times barricading themselves inside the house while strangers killed sheep, hogs and cattle outside. "Clouds and darkness are around us. The hand of the Almighty is laid in sore judgement upon us," she wrote. "We are a desolated & smitten people."

For Georgians, Sherman's march was the most famous and terrible event of their state's history, the last great act of war, the first act of Reconstruction and the symbol of more than a decade of human distress. But Sherman's "march from Atlanta to the sea" was really

General Sherman set up his headquarters at the mansion
of Charles Green, an English-born cotton merchant, built
in 1853. *Library of Congress*

General Sherman's guards and visitors loll in the entrance
hall of Charles Green's mansion in Savannah, December,
1864. *Drawing by Alfred Waud, Library of Congress*

only one part of a more important expedition which began at Chatta-nooga, Tennessee, in May, 1864, and which ended near Durham, North Carolina, in April, 1865. Indeed, Sherman's army faced sustained resistance only in the mountains of north Georgia before it reached Atlanta, and Sherman's men were able to march beyond Atlanta to the coast without opposition. Despite the celebrated destruction of Georgia, the federal force inflicted greater damage, with far greater personal vindictiveness, in South Carolina, the hated birthplace of secession. In fact, the damage done by Sherman's army extended over only a small part of Georgia, and most of the state remained untouched by physical warfare. The march was most important as a political triumph, conceived by a military man who distrusted politicians all his life, and as a glimpse of ruthless twentieth-century total war, directed by a man who was himself insecure and plagued with failure. Though the effects of Sherman's march were computed in terms of miles and tons of physical destruction, the greatest effects of the march were upon the people of the South and Georgia in particular. Though the march caused Georgians to remember the years of civil war and Reconstruction as a depressing, destructive time, Sherman's march was really the pivot point for an era which brought the industrial revolution to Georgia and which gave political power to the middle class for the first time, two exhilarating, constructive social developments.

On January 21, 1865, General Sherman's army crossed the Savannah River into South Carolina and left Georgia behind in a sea of confusion. After the fall of Richmond, the Confederate government fled south, held its final meeting at Washington, Georgia, and Jefferson Davis was arrested near Irwinville on May 10. Governor Brown, Vice-President Stephens, Senator Benjamin Hill, General Howell Cobb were also arrested. Major Henry Wirz, commander of Andersonville Prison, was hanged at Washington. Robert Toombs fled to Europe until it was safe to return. Defeated soldiers were straggling home on foot, eating raw turnips, meat skins, parched corn, anything they could find. John Kennaway, who followed Sherman's tracks in 1865, found ruins of homes at Calhoun, blank walls and skeleton houses at Marietta, a landscape littered with broken wagons, spent ammunition, abandoned breastworks, graves and carcasses of rotting horses. But he reflected that the greatest evidence of disaster was not the ruined property or ravaged countryside, but the faces of the ruined, ravaged people of Georgia: "I do not remember to have seen a smile upon a single human face."

On April 30, General Johnston telegraphed Governor Brown that hostilities with the United States had ceased, and federal authority, already established at Macon and Savannah, was extended over the whole state during April, May and June. In May, President Johnson proclaimed James Johnson, a Columbus lawyer, the provisional governor and instructed him to call a convention of "loyal Georgians" to form a new government. In October the convention met, repealed the secession ordinance, abolished slavery and repudiated the Confederate war debt. In November, Charles Jenkins, a judge who had been a Unionist before the war, was elected governor, and a new state legislature ratified the Thirteenth Amendment and passed laws which guaranteed the civil equality of freedmen. In March, 1867, Congress passed, over the President's veto, the military reconstruction act. Georgia's first government was abolished and the state was returned to military rule. Again the state government was reorganized, with more blacks included and more whites excluded. In April, 1868, Rufus Bullock was elected governor, and in July the new legislature ratified the Fourteenth Amendment. In 1869 the Republican governor quarrelled with the conservative legislature. In December, 1869, the United States Congress again imposed military control over Georgia and the

Henry Wirz, the commander at Andersonville Prison, was hanged at Washington in 1865. *Library of Congress*

Truce boats exchanging prisoners on the Savannah River,
April, 1865. *Drawing by William Waud, Library of
Congress*

state government was reconstructed for a third time. The new legislature, which included many Negroes and Republicans who had been excluded formerly, finally ratified the Fifteenth Amendment, which guaranteed Negro suffrage. Georgia was formally readmitted to the United States in July, 1870.

Though it took more than five years for Georgia to return to the Union, Georgians had quickly regained control of their own affairs. Georgia was reconstructed three times precisely because the conservatives in the state were so powerful. The very first legislature in 1865, in a daring demonstration of strength, elected Alexander Stephens, former Vice-President of the Confederacy, and Herschel V. Johnson, former Confederate senator, to the United States Senate and seven former Confederate military officers to the U. S. House of Representatives. In October, 1866, the legislature refused to ratify the Fourteenth Amendment, which would have secured Negro civil rights. In the April, 1868, legislature, radicals and Democrats were about equally represented, and relatively few white voters had been disfranchised at this time. In September, the legislature expelled its Negro members, three state senators and twenty-five representatives. In November, the Republicans were not able to carry Georgia for Grant. In March, 1869, the state senate rejected the Fifteenth Amendment, although the house narrowly ratified it. Though the freedmen exercised a political voice briefly in 1867 and 1868, the vigilante activities of the Ku Klux Klan subdued any political revolution by blacks in Georgia. Freedmen wandered to the cities to test freedom in 1866 and 1867, but they returned to plantations as renters and croppers, and social life resumed its accustomed pace and place. In the December, 1870, election the Democrats won overwhelming control of the state legislature. Faced with probable impeachment by an angry conservative legislature, Governor Bullock resigned his office and fled from Georgia in October, 1871.

5. Farmers and Businessmen

Henry Grady, editor of the Atlanta *Constitution* and spokesman of the industrialized, liberalized New South in the 1880's. *Atlanta Constitution*

"WHAT a radiant and charming and accomplished man he was!" exclaimed Josephus Daniels, the famous North Carolina journalist, after he had met Henry Grady, the aggressive young editor of the Atlanta *Constitution* during the prosperous 1880's. Grady was a public-spirited journalist and builder of one of the great newspapers of the South. A brilliant orator, Grady became the most acclaimed southerner of his day to plead for sectional reconciliation and regional reform after the Civil War. For nearly a decade, between 1880 when he purchased an interest in the *Constitution* and 1889 when he died unexpectedly, Grady wrote and spoke of economic achievement in a poverty-stricken land, of political harmony to a generation of Georgians who had suffered conquest and occupation, and he spoke of justice for the Negro in a society where slavery had been ended only recently and reluctantly. He was a compelling representative figure, a young Southern man who stood on the threshold of maturity and faced a world which had been transformed since his childhood against the wishes of his society. Grady was, indeed, a true regional patriot, for he voiced the deep, frustrated hopes of Southern people to rejoin the mainstream of American life. The New York *Times* called him "the great interpreter of a new spirit which was awakening the South, exhorting the people to concern themselves no longer about what they had lost, but to busy themselves with what they might find to do, to consecrate the past if they would, but to put

The commercial center of Atlanta, pictured in *Harper's Weekly*, February 19, 1887. *New York Public Library*

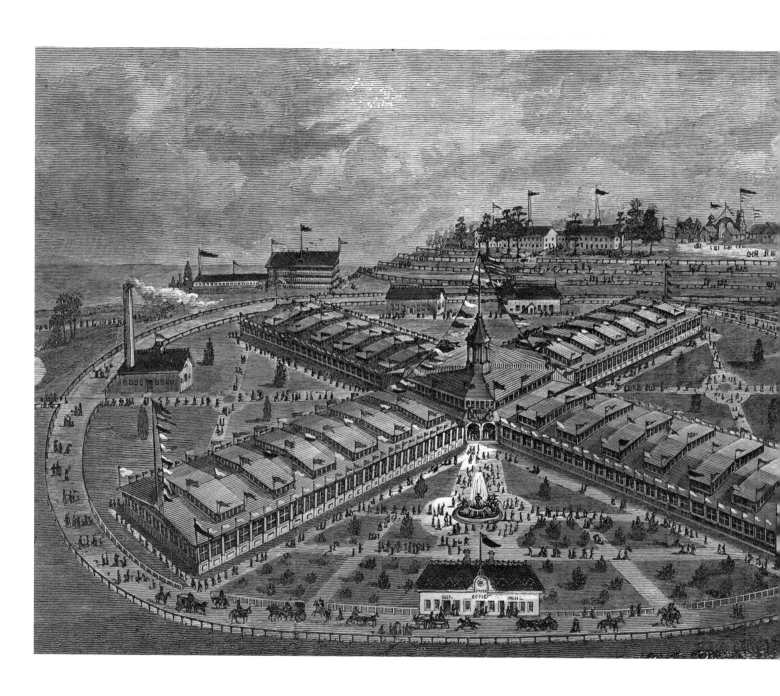

International Cotton Exposition at Atlanta, 1881, from
an illustrated newspaper of the period.
Private Collection

the whole strength of their minds and bodies into the building up of a New South."

A real social and political revolution had taken place in Georgia during the years of war and reconstruction. The Civil War had brought the industrial revolution to the South, and Reconstruction brought power to the middle class. In 1857 Joseph E. Brown, a pugnacious lawyer, once a farmer from north Georgia, had been elected governor and subsequently was reelected three more times during the war, an achievement unprecedented in the state's history. A self-made, professional man from a part of Georgia populated by independent mountaineers, who appealed to the common people for support, Brown's political success represented a shift of power from the old planters of middle Georgia. The vote for secession had been not only a defense of slavery but an assertion of economic independence for a region struggling to advance beyond a frontier, colonial status in national life. The reorganization of state government after 1865 specifically eliminated most of the old leading class—military officers above the rank of colonel, Confederate officials and men whose worth exceeded twenty thousand dollars.

The course of events during the war strengthened this new middle class at the expense of the planter class. The rapid inflation and depreciation of the currency benefitted people with debts and penalized people with money in the bank. The war destroyed the value of bank stock, railroad shares, land, slaves and Confederate bonds and currency, the wealth of rich men during the war. In the aftermath of Sherman's march, the planters were left without liquid capital or reliable labor. During the late 1860's the acreage under cultivation, the size of farm units, the value of land and crop production all declined in Georgia. At the same time, the value of taxable property in towns and cities increased from $38,000,000 to $55,000,000 between 1867 and 1872. Between 1860 and 1870 the value of farms in Georgia decreased from $157,072,803 to $94,559,468, and the value of farm machinery and equipment decreased from $6,844,387 to $4,614,701. During the same interval, the number of industrial establishments increased from 1,890 to 3,836, invested capital rose from $10,890,875 to $13,930,125, yearly industrial production expanded from $16,925,564 to $31,196,115. While the planters had been weakened, a new class of rich men whose wealth did not rest on land and slaves was strengthened.

Atlanta, which had been created and destroyed by the war, was a scene of amazing recovery. In the midst of crumbling walls, solitary chimneys and charred timbers, the city was fast rebuilding. Sidney Andrews described the scene in November, 1865: "From all this ruin and devastation a new city is springing up with marvellous rapidity. The streets are alive from morning 'till night with drays and carts and hand-barrows and wagons, hauling teams and shouting men, with loads of lumber and loads of brick and loads of sand, with piles of furniture and hundreds of packed boxes, with mortar-makers and carpenters and masons, with rubbish removers and house-builders, with a never-ending throng of pushing and crowding and scrambling and eager and excited and enterprising men, all bent on building and trading and swift fortune-making." People were living in shacks and tents, establishing stores in half-roofed houses. In 1867 a Milledgeville newspaper complained: "Atlanta is certainly a fast place in every sense of the word, and our friends in Atlanta are a fast people. They live fast, and they die fast. They make money fast, and they spend it fast. To a stranger, the whole city seems to be running on wheels, and all of the inhabitants continually blowing off steam." The center of Atlanta was described in December, 1865, by a visitor: "The middle of the city is a great open space of irregular shape, a wilderness of mud, with a

A bustling, and somewhat messy, Atlanta in 190
Atlanta Historical Society

confused jumble of railway sheds, and traversed by numberless rails, rusted and splashed, where strings of dirty cars are standing, and engines constantly puff and . . . resounds with the noise of carpenters and engines." Elizabeth Sterchi, a middle-aged Swiss schoolteacher who found herself in Georgia in 1868, called Atlanta "the great Babylon," overrun at night with rowdy men and bawdy women. "Atlanta is crowded with poor people piled one on another, perfect heathen in a civilized country. . . . The God of Atlanta," she wrote, "is money." Atlanta's business leaders were a new breed of middle-class industrialists and professional men, while the older generation of agrarian statesmen were aristocrats and conservative landowners. Atlanta was promoted as "a new place—modern, democratic—a fresh production, wholly practical, without antiquities or prejudices." Atlanta's population increased from thirty-seven thousand in 1880 to ninety thousand in 1900. Early in its history, during the Civil War and New South, Atlanta had already become the confident, progressive, boastful and materialistic city that it remains today.

Joseph E. Brown urged the people to accept each new plan of Congressional Reconstruction, no matter how repugnant or severe the terms and no matter how expedient the cooperation, on the grounds that recovery in the future was more important than loyalty to a lost past. The new promoters conspired with the Republicans who brought power with them to Atlanta. In 1867 the governor of the Third Military District brought his headquarters from Montgomery to Atlanta. In 1868 the Republican administration moved the state capital from Milledgeville to Atlanta. The city's industrialists were financial partners with political leaders who were hated by most Georgians. Hannibal Kimball, who came to Georgia from Chicago in 1866, became the city's most famous tycoon, constructing a new state capitol and an elegant hotel in Atlanta. Republican Governor Bullock issued state bonds worth more than thirty million dollars to finance Kimball's

The market place of a Georgia village during the cotton season, *Harper's Weekly*, February 12, 1887. *Private Collection*

railroads. The new leaders of Atlanta welcomed the return of Republicans to the city after the end of Reconstruction, and even Bullock was able to return to Atlanta and resume his business career in later years, despite charges of corruption which forced him to flee Georgia in 1871. Joe Brown announced in the North that his state wanted a great importation of "Yankee energy, Yankee enterprise, Yankee education, and Yankee business sense." In 1881 Atlanta became the scene of an International Cotton Exposition, designed to promote industry and investment in Georgia. The most famous stockholder of that enterprise, the man most celebrated and lionized when he reached Atlanta, was former General William T. Sherman. At last, the forces of economic and social change which came to Georgia during the Civil War and Reconstruction years had produced this happy, if ironic, reconciliation.

Money meant power, and power meant money. Grady's *Constitution* moralized: "Business is the biggest thing in this country. When the princes of commerce and industry say to the politicians that they must let dangerous experiments alone they will be heard and obeyed. Politicians may talk, but businessmen will act, control and dominate the destinies of this common sense country." Grady expressed this philosophy another way when he said, "The New South represents a perfect democracy, the oligarchs leading in the popular movement." "Atlanta is now the political power of the state concentrated in the hands of a few men," their critics cried. "Is Atlanta the state? And are the people willing to submit to the concentration of power in Atlanta and to the monopoly of all the important offices in the hands of a few men?" The new Atlanta ring was led by former Governor Joseph E. Brown, Confederate General John B. Gordon and planter-businessman Alfred H. Colquitt, with Henry Grady their spokesman. Colquitt and Gordon each served two terms as governor; between 1872 and

Cotton market scene, probably Marietta, c. 1900
Georgia Department of Archives and History

Unidentified rural Georgia family, c. 1900.
University of Georgia Library

1890 Brown or Gordon held one of Georgia's Senate seats and, after the end of his second term as governor in 1882, Colquitt held the other. Two splinter political groups—the Independents of the 1870's, led by William H. Felton, and the Populists of the 1890's, led by Tom Watson—challenged but failed to upset this domination of Georgia politics by the Atlanta machine. Although Brown and Colquitt died in 1894 and Gordon retired in 1895, they were followed by other politicians devoted to cities and industries. In 1904 opposition to the Atlanta machine reached a low when Governor Joseph M. Terrell was reelected without opposition. So great was the concentration of power in Atlanta during these years that a small Georgia newspaper complained: "As we are so far out here in the backwoods, we never hear what is going on at the capital until the thing is over with." Georgia humorist Bill Arp chided gently: "Our folks don't know what we are doing. Now Joe Brown is building a railroad right along in front of my house, and nobody knows it but me and him and his partners."

Henry Grady promised that the South was progressing confidently toward a bright rainbow of economic success and social stability just beyond a beckoning horizon: "A vision of surpassing beauty unfolds before my eyes. I see a South, the home of fifty millions of people, who rise up every day to call from blessed cities, vast hives of industry and thrift; her countrysides the treasures from which their resources are drawn; her streams vocal with whirring spindles; her valleys tranquil in the white and gold of the harvest, her rulers honest and her people loving, her homes happy and their hearthstones bright, her wealth diffused and poor-house empty; her two races walking together in peace and contentment; sunshine everywhere all the time." But Grady's words, no matter how sincere or well intentioned, were not the reality of Georgia life after the Civil War. If Grady's fame rests on unfulfilled promises, that was because he was sincerely optimistic by nature and because he died before he could put his words into action. Woodrow Wilson, that young lawyer in Atlanta, challenged Grady's credibility in 1886: "Papers like the *Constitution*, though they may represent fairly well the opinion of the politicians, do not represent anybody else." Tom Watson, spokesman for the unhappy farmers of the 1890's, cursed what he called "the splendid phraseology of silver-tongued orators from the city . . . the inspired clap-trap of some of its politicians and editors." The opposition in Georgia cried out against widespread poverty, demoralization, crime and misery. Frustrated veterans remembered these years, not as a time of pride and hope, but as an era when the great mass of Georgia people, both black and white, suffered most desperately on the land, when the state government was manipulated by cynical city politicians, when these cumulative frustrations and disappointments turned human relations toward an embittered crisis.

When Sidney Andrews visited Atlanta in 1865, he found the attitude of its citizens recklessly independent: "They point to the railroads centering here and say that if the country around was poorer and less productive, the mere storage and trans-shipment of freight would suffice to make Atlanta a great city." Truly, for the next seventy-five years Atlanta would continue to grow and prosper, not because of Georgia's wholesome social and economic development, but in spite of the state's languishing condition. Northern cotton mills did not come to Georgia in significant numbers until after 1900, and industrial diversification did not arrive until after World War II. Between 1880 and 1900, the number of people working at manufacturing jobs in the South rose only from 4.6 percent to 6.3 percent of the population. Like Jeeter Lester in Erskine Caldwell's *Tobacco Road*, most Georgia people remained on the land, farming, mining or fishing: "The spring-

A country girl coming from the market, from *Outing*,
October, 1903. *New York Public Library*

time . . . knows you got to stay on the land to feel good. God made the land. I stay where God made a place for me." In 1900, eighty-five percent of Georgia's population still lived on farms or in small villages, and sixty percent worked in agriculture. The farm force in Georgia actually increased from 336,000 in 1870 to more than 500,000 in 1900. In 1930 for every Southerner engaged in manufacturing and mechanical pursuits, there were still three in Southern farming. And most of these farmers—at least three-quarters of them in Georgia—continued to raise cotton by a primitive technique which had not changed since the early nineteenth century, one man and his family and a mule devoting all their energies to raising a small patch of cotton. As soon as one crop had been picked, it was time to prepare the ground for a new crop. Despite the new South's preaching about agricultural reform, Southern farmers continued to raise cotton and too much of it. Edward King's observations at Savannah in 1875 were a troubling echo of the cotton preoccupation which had impoverished the South before the Civil War: "We were amazed at the masses of cotton bales piled everywhere. They lined the commercial avenues for hundreds and hundreds of rods; down by the waterside they were heaped in mammoth piles, and the procession of drays seemed endless. The huge black ships swallowed bale after bale; the clank of the hoisting crane was heard from morning till night. At the great stone Custom House the talk was of cotton; at the old Exchange cotton was the theme; and in all the offices from end to end of Bay Street, we encountered none save busy buyers and factors, worshipping the creamy staple and gossiping rapturously of profits possible."

After the deaths of white soldiers and emancipation of black slaves, the greatest practical effect of the Civil War in the South was a shortage of capital and labor. All of the assets of Southerners—Confederate bonds and currency, bank stock, slaves and land—had been

Georgia villagers at a country store, from *Outing*, October, 1903. *New York Public Library*

depleted or destroyed by the war. Over the countryside of Georgia, landowners did not have the cash money to hire laborers, and farmers did not have the means to rent farms. So a new system of sharecropping evolved naturally to serve the mutual needs of these people. If a farmer had no money and few implements of agriculture, his landlord could furnish him not only land and a house to live in, but also food, tools, mules. And at the end of the planting season they would share the harvest between them. The worker would be credited with his share of the cotton and charged with all supplies he had received during the year plus the rent of the land. By 1870 sharecropping had already become common in middle Georgia, and the system spread with agricultural distress across the cotton belt of the Old South, first among the blacks and later among the whites. In 1880, 36.2 percent of all Southern farms were operated by sharecroppers. By 1920, 55 percent of all Southern farms in the ten chief cotton states were farmed by tenants; in 1925, 57.7 percent were tenants; by 1930, 61.5 percent were tenants. Of the 255,598 farm operators in Georgia in 1930, 70,596 owned their land, 9,206 were part owners, 1,406 were managers, 27,533 were cash renters and 146,857 were sharecroppers. The cash renters and sharecroppers, people who did not own the land which was the only means of their support, represented 68.2 percent of Georgia farmers in 1930.

Erskine Caldwell looked into the faces of these Southern sharecroppers during the Depression and saw a look of desperate hope in their eyes: "Every one of them was waiting for the cotton to mature. They believed in cotton. They believed in it as some men believe in God. They had faith in the earth and in the plants that grow in the earth. Even though they had been fooled the year before, and for many years before that, they were certain the fields would soon be showered with tumbling, bursting bolls of glistening white cotton." Perversely,

A one-room school, Randolph County, c. 1900.
Georgia Department of Archives and History

cotton was the one staple crop raised in America which contributed nothing directly consumable to the farm family, and the preoccupation with cotton meant that the necessary foods were not being raised. The farms of the New South tended to be less and less self-supporting, compared with the farms and plantations of the Old South, which produced most of their subsistence needs. In 1920 Georgia farm families purchased more than one-half of their food and feed stock from outside of the state. One-crop cotton cultivation contributed to soil erosion. People who rented other people's land would make few improvements on property they did not own; instead, they would squeeze all they could from the soil each year, hoping to move the next season to more fertile fields. A sample study made in 1933 suggested that one-third of all Southern land was eroded and that at least one-half of all eroded land in the United States was in the South.

The one desperate hope of these sharecroppers was to raise a little more cotton, somehow, and sell it at a little higher price and get out of debt. But new, cheap and more productive cotton-producing areas were opening up in the southwestern United States and other parts of the world. From 1860 to 1900, aided by the Homestead Law and the general movement of the American people, total farm acreage in the United States increased 400,000,000 acres. Georgia and the Old South, with worn-out land, little capital and a rigid tradition of one-mule farm cultivation, could not compete in a glutted market, where the only way to survive was to produce large quantities of cheap cotton. Cotton prices continued to decline from a dollar a pound after the Civil War, to twenty-five cents in 1868, to twelve cents in the 1870's, to nine cents in the 1880's, to seven cents in the 1890's. Debts that could have been repaid with ten bales of cotton in 1889 had to be repaid with eighteen bales of cotton five years later. By 1892 there would be a worldwide surplus of 13,000,000 bales of cotton which could not be

Blacksmith, Irwin County, 1935.
Arthur Rothstein, Library of Congress

sold. A further catastrophe for the cotton farmer was the boll weevil, an insect which appeared in Texas in 1894 and began travelling eastward at the rate of seventy-five to a hundred miles per year. The weevil, which destroyed cotton bolls, reached Georgia about 1915. Cotton production, which had been 1,660,000 bales in 1919, plummeted to only 588,000 bales in 1923. This crisis, with the coming of the Depression, was a final disaster from which the small farmer could not recover. Ironically, New Deal farm programs tended to benefit the owners of land and large farmers, not sharecroppers. Acreage or production controls just put farm laborers out of work, while the landowners pocketed federal aid.

For Georgia's suffering cotton farmers, a larger harvest might mean only a smaller income, further accumulating debts and ultimate disaster. Farmers became dependent from harvest to harvest on credit at any terms. A farmer might secure his loans with his farm land until, after years of mounting debts, he would be compelled to sell the land. Then the farmer, now working on another man's land, would have to borrow money secured by his future crop. Creditors, who knew that cotton was not perishable, valued it as loan security, and, perversely, an indebted farmer would find his credit measured by how much more cotton he could produce. This crop lien system encouraged farmers to raise more one-crop cotton, despite its falling price in a glutted market; to sell it immediately even if higher prices could be found by delaying the sale; and to continue credit purchasing from the local merchant or plantation owner at inflated prices and high interest rates. So at the end of this credit conundrum, an unfortunate cotton farmer might find himself without land and, mortgaged to more cotton production, without even the free will to abandon his farm or cotton cultivation. These poor men were slowly, inevitably sinking in the economic quicksand of one-crop cotton, sterile and eroded soil, overproduction, de-

Plowing an eroded field, Heard County, 1941.
Jack Delano, Library of Congress

Unidentified couple, August, 1936.
Margaret Bourke-White, Syracuse University Library

clining prices, small cash incomes, cumulative debts, ultimate im-
poverishment.

By the Depression the cotton belt of the South would become, as
it was described at the time, "a miserable panorama of unpainted
shacks, rain-gullied fields, straggling fences, rattle-trap Fords, dirt,
poverty, disease, drudgery and monotony that stretches for a thousand
miles." A New Deal study portrayed with statistical coolness the life
of a tenant family during the Depression: most tenants lived in unpainted four-room shacks; sanitation was most primitive; eighty percent of the homes were supplied with water from wells; the average
income per capita was $73 per year, $309 for the average family; one-
third of this income was in the form of foods raised for the family,
chickens, eggs, pigs, syrup, corn, peas, sweet potatoes; another third
of the income was used, $13 monthly, to buy food, flour, lard, salt
pork, kerosene, medicines; the last third of the family income was
spent for clothing; there was no money left for household improvements or repairs. In 1930, 2.1 percent of Georgia farms had tractors,
2.9 percent had electric lights, 3.1 percent had piped water. In 1934,
there were 3,344 licensed midwives in Georgia, mostly black women,
who delivered 42 percent of Georgia's children. Between 1920 and
1940, the large majority of southerners, black and white, lived barely
above the minimum subsistence level on a diet of meal, molasses and
meat, reminiscent of slavery days. All of these raw facts define a world
without adequate sanitation, doctors or hospitals, secure homes. They
define a confining world of malnutrition, pellagra, rickets, hookworm,
unnecessary sickness, lassitude, large families, further distress, frustra-
tion and greater misery.

Georgia's farmers had, since the colony's early dependence on
England, produced raw materials for outsiders, who sold them manufactured goods in return. Over two hundred years the natural re-

sources of the frontier "colony" had been depleted with no capital accumulated within the South to replace the potential productivity which was being extracted from the land and forests of the region. The only way the people of the exhausted frontier could maintain their standard of living would be to become pioneers and blaze their way into new territory. It was exactly this crisis at the end of the eighteenth century which had brought settlers to Georgia from North Carolina and Virginia, where their lands had been exhausted by tobacco farming. Another similar crisis during the early nineteenth century had forced many small farmers of Georgia to move to Alabama and Mississippi, the new frontier of the 1830's. Between 1865 and 1875 some fifty thousand small farmers, half white and half black, had left Georgia for the fresh cotton fields of Arkansas and Texas, the latest frontier. Each time—1780, 1830 and 1870—the farmers of frontier Georgia had been able to support themselves, after the depletion of the natural resources, forests cut down and land wasted, by moving to a new territory. But after the 1890's, when the American frontier finally closed, the farmers who remained in Georgia and the other states of the Old South were truly stranded at last, with no place to go except to the cities. A great exodus of blacks to Northern cities began during World War I, and whites began moving to Southern cities during the 1920's and the Depression. Between 1920 and 1930, some 266,000 people abandoned 55,000 farms, or 3,400,000 acres of farm land, in Georgia.

The depleted South, still after, as before, the Civil War, remained a "colony" of the industrialized North. Outsiders with accumulated capital even took over control of the marketing of the precious cotton crop—farmers were indebted to planters who were indebted to seaport factors who were really agents of these men. The South continued to produce cheap raw materials and buy costly manufactured goods. Henry Grady told a famous story of an elaborate Southern funeral,

Unidentified Southern family, August, 1936.
Margaret Bourke-White, Syracuse University Library

Family at Dahlonega, August, 1936.
Margaret Bourke-White, Syracuse University Library

where only the corpse and the hole in the ground had been produced in Georgia. The greatest inducement for Northern industry to come to the South in the late nineteenth century was to exploit the region's raw materials and low wage scale. The "industries" which came to Georgia were cotton and lumber mills, the simplest kind of work which paid the lowest wages and depleted the natural resources. Symbolically, the ships coming to Savannah at the end of the nineteenth century often arrived in ballast, because there was no great consumer demand, but the ships steamed away low in the water with cotton, lumber and turpentine. Suggestively, in 1929 Southern industrial workers earned $844 compared with $1,364 in New England and $1,447 in the Middle Atlantic states. In 1940 Southern industries employed 17.3 percent of the nation's factory workers but paid them only 11.8 percent of the national factory wages.

The great enterprises of the region—coal, iron, steel, utilities, newspapers, chain stores, insurance companies—were largely controlled or owned outside the South. J. P. Morgan dominated the Southern Railway System, which he had created in 1894 from thirty separate corporations, one of which was the Central Railroad of Georgia. In 1900, the ten largest railroads in the South were controlled by Northerners, and seventy percent of their directors came from the North. More than ninety percent of the mileage of the thirty-one major Southern lines was controlled by Northern interests in 1900. Under a system of differentiated freight rates, which had grown up during the late nineteenth century and continued until a ruling by the Interstate Commerce Commission in 1939, it cost about thirty-nine percent more to ship manufactured goods in the South than in New England, a practice which tended to keep the South producing raw materials and discouraged the establishment of new small manufacturers in the region. Under a similar system of differentiated prices for iron and steel products—like the famous Pittsburgh Plus, by which Southern consumers paid a premium price, representing the cost of making steel at Pittsburgh plus the theoretical cost of shipping it to Georgia—the established manufacturers were protected from cheap regional competition, Southern prices for steel and iron hardware and plate were raised, and Southern industrialization was effectively retarded. Like British aristocrats visiting their Crown colonies in another era, some of the nation's most wealthy and powerful industrialists spent their winter holidays in Georgia, completing this impressionistic sketch of the state's colonial status after the Civil War: the Vanderbilts and Morgans at their private hunting preserve on Jekyll Island, the Carnegies at their splendid stone castle on wilderness Cumberland Island, Henry Ford at his Richmond Hill plantation, Mark Hanna at Thomasville, a fashionable retreat where he offered William McKinley the chance to become President in 1896.

By the end of the nineteenth century, most of the people of Georgia, who remained unhappy farmers living close to the land and outside the industrial system, who had heard so much propaganda about big business but still lived impoverished lives across the undeveloped countryside, sensed vaguely that they had been swindled by the business promoters and politicians. During Henry Grady's lifetime, Henry Watterson of Louisville, another Southern journalist and New South publicist, had cautioned: "All the robber baron theories, which have amassed unequal and ill-gained fortunes in the East, are dinned in the ears of the honest, but impoverished, South. Mr. Grady should throw himself across the bridle path of this fallacy. If he does not, he will see the day when the best blood of the South will feed the factories which grind out squalor to millions and millions for masters as cruel and rapacious as ever trod New England soil." Tom Watson, the spokesman for Georgia's unhappy farmers during the 1890's, rejected the

Tom Watson, U.S. Congressman and reformer-turned-reactionary. *University of Georgia*

A farm couple at Locket, August, 1936.
Margaret Bourke-White from You Have Seen Their
Faces *(New York, 1937) with permission*

A farm couple at Maiden Lane, August, 1936.
Margaret Bourke-White from You Have Seen Their
Faces *(New York, 1937) with permission*

New South leaders' faith in industrialization and nationalism: "Ever since the close of the Civil War there has been heard the cry, 'We must encourage Northern capital to come South.' We have got down on our knees to the Northern capitalist, and in almost every instance he has been enabled to dictate his own terms. All over the South, when Northern capital puts up a factory, builds a railroad, opens a bank, develops a quarry, sinks a shaft of the Oil Trust, it has been shrewd enough to take into copartnership a sufficient number of Southern men eager to make money. It has taken in Southern editors, whose newspapers need financial support; leading lawyers hungry for good fees, ambitious politicians who need campaign funds, and thus a fictitious sentiment has been created in our midst which sanctions the system under which we suffer."

In 1906 these discontented Georgia farmers at last staged a successful political revolt, when Hoke Smith, the self-proclaimed representative of the common rural folk against the city politicians and industrialists, was elected governor. His election signalled a victory for the farmers and inaugurated a half century, until 1962, during which rural politicians would dominate Georgia government. In 1908 the state Democratic party adopted a county unit system, which gave small rural counties a commanding voice in the choice of governors and senators. Under this system of indirect nomination, each county had a specified number of votes; nominations would be determined by unit, not popular, votes; unit votes of a county would go to the candidate with a popular plurality in the county; the eight most populous counties were entitled to six unit votes, the next 30 largest counties were entitled to four each; and the other 121 counties were entitled to two each. A few votes in a sparsely populated county could nullify thousands of votes in an urban county. A unit vote could represent 938 people in a small county or 92,721 in a large one. So the successful politicians of Georgia between 1908 and 1962 made their appeal to rural voters, playing on their fear of change, big government, cities, industries and Negroes.

In April, 1913, the raped and battered body of thirteen-year-old Mary Phagan was found in the basement of the Atlanta pencil factory where she worked. Her employer, Leo M. Frank, a Northerner from Brooklyn, a Jew and an industrialist, was arrested, convicted and sentenced to death. After two years of unsuccessful appeals, Governor John M. Slaton commuted the death sentence to life imprisonment. Meanwhile, Tom Watson and others had been calling for Frank's death. In August, 1915, a mob took Frank from the state prison at Milledgeville and hung him from an oak tree in Marietta. (Many years later, a witness came forward exonerating Leo Frank.)

After the death of Tom Watson in 1922, a young lawyer from McRae named Eugene Talmadge, who sported red suspenders and white shirtsleeves as his badge of identity with the common man, became the spokesman and representative of the rural people and farmers of Georgia. A candidate for every statewide Democratic party nomination except one between 1926 and 1946—three times for commissioner of agriculture, two for U.S. senator, five times for governor—he was elected four times governor, more than any other man except Joseph E. Brown. Talmadge, who boasted that he would never campaign in a town large enough to have trolley cars, said that God made grass for cows to eat and not for city people to chop off with lawn mowers. In 1932 Talmadge received 118 more unit votes than his seven opponents, though they received 43,000 more popular votes. In 1946 he received more county unit votes but fewer popular votes than his rival, James V. Carmichael, an Atlanta attorney and industrialist. Talmadge preached the old-fashioned virtues of thrift, hard work, individualism, low taxes, small government. The effect of the county

Gene Talmadge, four-term Governor of Georgia in 1930's and 1940's and representative of the common man. *Atlanta Constitution*

The lynching of Leo Frank in August, 1915, reflected Georgians' fear of outsiders and businessmen. *Georgia Department of Archives and History*

Hull, Georgia, August, 1936.
Margaret Bourke-White, Syracuse University Library

unit system, which gave him power, was to make Georgia politics unresponsive to the needs of the city people, with the new ideas they were adopting in their mobile, middle-class lives. Talmadge in the depths of the Depression prevented Georgia from participating fully in New Deal relief programs, because he feared big government and social programs for Negroes.

Lester Maddox, a cafeteria owner who refused at pistol-point to serve two Negro divinity students in his eatery the day after President Johnson signed the Civil Rights Act of 1964, was another spokesman for the fears and insecurities of rural people. Maddox, whose father had moved to Atlanta from the devastated Georgia countryside to labor in an Atlanta steel mill, was a hard-working, self-made man, proud of his property rights and resentful of welfare programs for people who could not, or in his view would not, make it on their own. In 1966, running for governor, Maddox ran second to his Republican opponent but became governor when, no candidate receiving a majority of the votes, the Democrat-controlled legislature selected him. Like Watson and Talmadge, Maddox was a backward-looking reactionary who believed devoutly and sincerely in Thomas Jefferson's eighteenth-century system of sturdy farmers and bucolic pastures, and so could not lead the people of Georgia smoothly into a twentieth-century world of cities and industries. Significantly, Georgia's three most progressive modern governors—Ellis Arnall in the 1940's, Carl Sanders in the 1960's and Jimmy Carter in the 1970's—were not particularly popular throughout the state, perhaps because they were unwilling to indulge the prejudices and fears of rural voters. Halfway through the twentieth century, Georgia was still more isolated and not more united with the main currents of national life, and the South still the poorest and least progressive section of the land. It had not yet become the Georgia and New South of Henry Grady's noble vision in the 1880's.

Lester Maddox, segregationist Governor, 1968. *UPI/Bettmann*

6. Blacks and Whites

THE late 1860's were years of change, confusion and turbulence that would aggravate the inevitable fears and resentments between the defeated whites and long-enslaved blacks. During the first year or two after the war, freedmen wandered into towns to test their independence. Despite efforts of the Freedmen's Bureau to feed and clothe them and protect their rights, the blacks soon discovered that the government would give them little work or land. After a winter or two of homelessness and starvation, most freedmen returned to plantations. Now they were paid monthly wages, but they were often living in the same cabins, working in the same fields under the same drivers from slavery days — and again dependent upon a white man's good will.

Protected for a time by a Republican state government and agents of the Freedmen's Bureau, the blacks had two or three years to exercise their new right to vote. The state government was thrice reorganized by the U.S. Congress, each time with the participation of more blacks and fewer whites. In the summer of 1868, with the approach of the presidential election, political agitation among blacks seemed particularly alarming to the whites. Ella Thomas of Augusta, the wife of a failed planter, predicted an uprising among the blacks: "The South feels instinctively that she is standing upon the mouth of a volcano. Four or five colored men said that the white folks are scared of the niggers, that things wasn't like they used to be and that they was gwine to have fine times and burn up every house along the road!"

242

Unidentified plantation scene, c. 1900.
From Rudolph Eickemeyer's Down South *(New York 1900), University of Georgia Library*

By 1868 masked patrollers—calling themselves "regulators," "jay-hawkers," "black horse cavalry" or "Ku Klux Klan"—began to frighten ignorant and superstitious freedmen into obedience by breaking into their houses at night, disguised with blackened faces or masks, blowing horns and waving guns. Uncooperative blacks who argued with whites, wanted to buy land a white wanted, courted a white woman, taught school to freedmen or voted for Republicans might be threatened, beaten or killed. Charles Smith of Walton County complained of a Klan visit in 1871: "I heard my wife hollering, 'Ku-Klux! Ku-Klux!' They knocked one door down. They beat me as long as they wanted to with rocks and pistols, and then they took a hickory and whipped me. Eight men struck me eight licks apiece on my bare back. They made my wife get down on her knees and stripped her dress down about her waist. They stripped my sister stark naked!" Back at work on plantations and their vote restricted by intimidation, blacks had already lost much of their new independence, uncertain even when protected by Federal soldiers.

After the end of Reconstruction the people of Georgia and the South were left to themselves to work out their social relations. The Freedmen's Bureau was closed in 1872, when a regular Democrat was elected governor of Georgia. Soon the social idealism of wartime was tarnished by the nation's industrialization, faith in laissez-faire, Social Darwinism, Anglo-Saxon nativism and foreign expansionism justified in part by "the white man's burden." In 1876 the U.S. Supreme Court ruled that the right of suffrage was not necessarily a part of American citizenship as provided in the Fifteenth Amendment. In 1883 the Court declared parts of the Civil Rights Act of 1875, guaranteeing equal accommodations to all regardless of race, as unconstitutional. In 1891 the defeat of Henry Cabot Lodge's bill for U.S supervision of national elections signalled an end of efforts to preserve black voting. In 1896 the Supreme Court ruled that public facilities could be separate

After the Civil War, most blacks returned to the same plantations, fields and houses where they had lived and worked during slavery days. Laborers at the Hermitage plantation, outside Savannah, c. 1890. *Library of Congress*

but equal. In 1895, 1897, 1902, and 1903 the Court refused to hear disfranchisement appeals from black citizens in the South. The sudden emancipation and enfranchisement of nearly one-half of Georgia's population, unprepared by no fault of their own for responsible citizenship, was a serious social problem. White Georgians wished to return the freedmen as much as possible to a productive, and humble, position. In 1879, the traveller Sir George Campbell, an Englishman who was not unsympathetic to the practical problems of rapid social and political change, quoted a Georgian who stated this determination more bluntly: "He thinks the negro first-rate to 'shovel dirt,' a function for which he was made, but no good for much else. He must be 'kept in his place,' as it is the fashion to say in Georgia."

Segregation laws had not, of course, been necessary during slavery days, and there was no rigid segregation in Georgia life and law until the 1890's. Though public schools, started just after the Civil War, had always been segregated, in most areas of daily living custom and choice regulated relations between blacks and whites. Across the state, inconsistency seemed to be the rule. In 1875 blacks could ride street-cars in Augusta and Atlanta but not in Savannah. Railroads usually provided one car for ladies and nonsmokers and another for blacks and smokers. By 1900 blacks could legally still do everything in Georgia except be buried in a white cemetery, marry a white girl, ride or sleep in white railroad cars or work on an integrated chain gang. As long as there was no pressure or opportunity for blacks to cross accepted lines and as long as old traditions of social life prevailed, there was no need for rigid segregation laws.

Emancipation was a fact and black people were making substantial progress between 1865 and 1900. By 1900 seven Negro colleges had been established in Georgia. Illiteracy among Georgia blacks dropped from 92.1 percent in 1870, to 81.6 percent in 1880, to 67.3 percent in 1890, to 52.4 percent in 1900. In Dougherty County landholding

Cotton porter at Savannah, c. 1885
J. N. Wilson, Private Collection

steadily increased from none in 1870, to 2,500 acres in 1880, to 10,000 acres in 1890, to 15,000 acres in 1898. By 1906 Georgia Negroes owned 1,400,000 acres of land and were assessed for $28,000,000 property. You could express all of these raw statistics by saying that 470,000 freedmen in Georgia increased their landholding by over a million acres and reduced their rate of illiteracy by fifty percent in one generation, a remarkable accomplishment.

During these same years, while the condition of blacks was advancing, the living standard of whites was regressing. Agents from Alabama and Mississippi plantations came to Georgia after the Civil War to hire Negro laborers, whose places on Georgia farms were filled by whites. As cotton prices declined and debts mounted, more and more whites were compelled to sell their land, then rent another man's land and, finally reduced to the last extremity, to become farm tenants or sharecroppers like the Negroes. A tenant cabin might house a Negro family one year and a white family the next. By 1900 there were more white tenant farmers than black tenants in Southern agriculture. By 1920 in the thirteen cotton producing states of the South, 61.2 percent of all tenants were white, and only 38.5 percent were black. After World War I the blacks abandoned the Southern countryside and moved to Northern cities, but the whites remained until the final collapse of Southern agriculture during the Depression. Between 1920 and 1935, 325,000 more whites became tenants in the South, while during the same interval 94,000 Negroes left their sharecropper farms. In Georgia, the number of white tenants increased from 63,317 in 1900, to 98,754 in 1930, to 101,649 in 1935; the number of black tenants increased from 71,243 in 1900 to 113,938 in 1920, decreased to 75,636 in 1930 and to 62,682 in 1935. By 1935 in the South nearly two-thirds of all farm tenants, renters and sharecroppers, were whites. Tenant farmers in the cotton belt of the South were computed in 1932 to be

Woman sifting rice, Saint Simon's Island, c. 1895.
Private Collection

OVERLEAF:
Cotton fields outside Savannah, c. 1885.
J. N. Wilson, University of Georgia Library

1,091,944 whites and 698,839 blacks. Thus a land tenure system which had helped to control Negro labor and keep him in his place after the Civil War had by the 1930's come to dominate nearly twice as many Southern whites as blacks.

In the face of their own alarming retrogression, the whites observed and feared this considerable Negro advancement in ownership, education and future prospects. Before his death in 1885, Robert Toombs pronounced: "As long as a Negro keeps his place I like him well enough. As a race, they are vastly inferior to whites and deserve pity. This pity I am willing to extend to them as long as they remain Negroes, but the moment a nigger tries to be a white man, I hate him like hell." A white man wrote during 1910 about the incipient crisis: "The differences between the races are growing more intense and troublesome. A few years ago the Negro was the laborer and the white men were 'bosses.' That has all changed now, and the two races are coming into close competition as renters and day laborers. The Negro has almost gone out of certain sections of our county, while whites have filled in and are doing the work." Forrest Pope, a working man in Atlanta, wrote in 1906: "All the genuine Southern people like the Negro as a servant, and so long as he remains strictly in what we choose to call his place, everything is all right. But when ambition, prompted by real education, causes the Negro to grow restless and bestir himself to get out of that servile condition, then there will be sure enough trouble . . . and I will kill him." Governor Allen Candler in 1901: "Do you know that you can stand on the dome of the capitol of Georgia and see more Negro colleges with endowments than you can see white schools? I do not believe in the higher education of the darky. He should be taught the trades, but when he is taught the fine arts he gets educated above his caste and it makes him unhappy."

The development of rigid segregation at the end of the nineteenth

Woman grinding rice, Saint Simon's Island, c. 1895
Private Collection

century was really an admission that the lives of most whites and blacks were converging and that hard lines would have to be drawn for the first time to separate them. In 1890 the Farm Alliance elected 160 of 219 members of the Georgia legislature, and in 1891 the legislature passed the state's first segregation law, a comprehensive bill which separated whites and blacks on railroads. This made Georgia the ninth state to adopt such a law. Further laws passed in 1891, 1897 and 1908 separated convicts on the chain gang and at penal camps. The Separate Parks Law of 1905 was the first state legislation seeking to segregate public amusements and recreation. This was the fulfillment of Henry Grady's own prescription voiced during the 1880's, that the two races must "walk in separate paths in the South. These paths should be made equal—but separate they must be now and always. This means separate schools, separate churches, separate accommodations everywhere . . . separate but equal, as near as may be." This separate but equal doctrine was affirmed by the Supreme Court in 1896.

Negroes had been granted the vote in 1867, but they never dominated the government of Georgia during Reconstruction. Only one black representative served the state in Congress, 1869–71. During the 1860's and 1870's, the black vote was largely eliminated or made ineffective by the Ku Klux Klan, night riders who flogged and threatened uncooperative freedmen. The election of a recognized Democrat as governor in 1872 signalled the conservatives' return to power, and the state legislature in 1873 changed residency requirements for voting from six months to a year in state elections and from thirty days to six months in county elections, a law directed against the transient Negro vote. Nevertheless, for the twenty-five years after 1880, the first post-Reconstruction election in which the Negro vote played a significant part, the black vote was alternately courted and cursed by every white

"The Freedmen's Bureau at Dr. Fuller's Plantation" from Whitelaw Reid, *A Southern Tour* (New York, 1866). *University of Georgia Library*

Coastal Georgia woman with her pipe, c. 1920. *Carl Julien, University of South Carolina Library*

faction. Each political contest threatened to divide the white voters and throw the balance of power to the blacks. This was more than theory in a state with 816,906 whites and 723,133 blacks in 1880. During the late nineteenth century, the conservative whites, who controlled the powerful newspapers and had money to buy the most votes, usually received the Negro vote. For example, in 1880 most Negroes voted for Alfred Colquitt, the machine candidate, and not the reform nominee, Thomas Norwood.

Georgia's unhappy farmers cried out in an angry crescendo of political revolt in the 1890's. In the 1890 elections, in six of the ten Congressional districts, conservatives lost their seats to candidates supported by the Farmers' Alliance. The Alliance took control of the state party convention, chose the governor, wrote the platform, elected three-fourths of the state senators and four-fifths of the state representatives. The state legislature proposed bills to extend the powers of the railroad commission, prohibit monopolistic business practices, regulate banking, reform the crop lien laws, prohibit speculation in farm products, extend the public school system. In 1894 these farmers, now calling themselves Populists, bolted the Democratic Party and appealed to the common interests of all poor Georgians, black and white. Their leader, Congressman Tom Watson, became their spokesman: "The colored tenant is in the same boat with the white tenant, the colored laborer with the white laborer. . . . The accident of color can make no difference in the interests of farmers, croppers and laborers. If you stand up for your rights and for your manhood, if you stand shoulder to shoulder with us in this fight . . . wipe out the color line and put every man on his citizenship irrespective of color."

This radical program, which recognized for the first time the essential mutual dependence of all poor Georgia farmers, was a revolutionary challenge, to which the machine Democrats responded with

A former slave woman learning to read, c. 1900. *From Rudolph Eickemeyer's* Down South *(New York, 1900), University of Georgia Library*

extreme defenses. Whites were told that if they did not vote a straight Democratic ticket, the Negroes would wield the balance of power. But those same Democrats corralled Negroes like sheep, bribed them with liquor and barbecue and herded them into voting places. Sandy Beaver remembered the famous election frauds of 1894: "I remember seeing wagon loads of Negroes brought into the wagon yards, the night before the election. There was whiskey for them, and all night many drank, sang and fought. But the next morning they were herded to the polls and openly paid . . . each man as he handed in his ballot." A Negro, paid ten cents a ballot, could make six dollars by voting sixty times. In the Tenth District the Democratic candidate for Congress received a majority of 13,780 votes out of a total possible poll that should have been no more than 11,240. The total vote cast in Augusta was twice the number of registered voters. Watson lost his seat in Congress, thanks to the cry of "Negro domination," the fear of Negroes which justified these election frauds, and he retired from politics for a decade. One good Democrat exclaimed after the 1894 elections: "We *had* to do it! Those damned Populists would have ruined the country!"

Henry Grady had written years before: "The worst thing, in my opinion, that could happen is that the white people of the South should stand in opposing factions, with the great mass of ignorant and purchasable Negro voters between them. If the Negro were skillfully led, it would give them the balance of power, a thing not to be considered. If their vote were not compacted [bought or suppressed], it would invite the debauching bid of factions and drift surely to that which was most corrupt and cunning." The Augusta *Chronicle*, like Grady's *Constitution* a voice for the regular Democrats and the industrialists, said it was a thousand times better for Georgia people to suffer the ills of the present than by division to open the South to a Negro menace.

Cooking and sewing classes at Atlanta University, c. 1890.
From Photogravures of Atlanta University *(Boston, 1900), University of Georgia Library*

Always dissident political groups were accused of inflaming a sea of black passion and violence, and fear of the Negro had been used to justify cheating in elections. So for two generations the Negro had become the effective, though passive, ally of the Democratic political machine against the unhappy farmers of Georgia, the great mass of the white people. Rebecca Felton, whose husband was run out of Georgia politics when he tried to champion Negro rights in the 1870's, reflected in later years: "The Negro and his future in politics became a bugbear—a scarecrow used by crafty office-seekers to infuriate the minds of Southern men and women. It was the clamp that held thousands of good men to the Democratic party after it was known to be dominated by industrial grafters." Tom Watson, frustrated and embittered by the election frauds of 1894, cursed them: "The fear of the Negro has hypnotized the Democratic voters into abject submission to the Corporation Ring. Negro Domination is their mainstay, their chief asset, their pet mascot, their never-ending means of striking terror into the souls of the whites and compelling them to swallow the Ring pill no matter how nasty. The argument against the independent political movement in the South may be boiled down to one word —niggers!"

For most white people in Georgia, the black man had become by 1900 the single most repugnant symbol of the false expectations and cruel frustrations of the New South era. As farm tenants and share-croppers, the common white farmers had become powerless to alter the direction of their lives, sinking under the pressure of one-crop cotton, sterile and eroded soil, overproduction, declining prices, low incomes and cumulative debts. They grew alarmed when they observed Negro progress after emancipation and compared it unfavorably with their own deteriorating lives. Rigid segregation evolved in the 1890's to protect these fearful whites who were losing their place in

The minstrel show, with white performers in blackface, mingled affection and ridicule of the black man. Terrell County in the 1920's. *Georgia Department of Archives and History*

Le Petit Journal

Le Petit Journal
CHAQUE JOUR — 6 PAGES — 5 CENTIMES
Administration : 61, rue Lafayette

Le Supplément illustré
CHAQUE SEMAINE 5 CENTIMES

5 Centimes SUPPLÉMENT ILLUSTRÉ **5** Centimes

Le Petit Journal Militaire, Maritime, Colonial..... 10 cent.
Le Petit Journal agricole, 5 cent. ✶ LA MODE du Petit Journal, 10 cent.
Le Petit Journal illustré de La Jeunesse..... 10 cent.
On s'abonne sans frais dans tous les bureaux de poste

ABONNEMENTS
	SIX MOIS	UN AN
SEINE ET SEINE-ET-OISE	2 fr.	3 fr. 50
DÉPARTEMENTS	2 fr.	4 fr. »
ÉTRANGER	2 50	5 fr. »

Les manuscrits ne sont pas rendus

Dix-septième année DIMANCHE 7 OCTOBRE 1906 Numéro 829

LES « LYNCHAGES » AUX ÉTATS-UNIS
Massacre de nègres à Atlanta (Georgie)

society, at the same time that most blacks and whites were converging in direct competition. The New South leaders had appealed for reform but had stifled any true popular reform, with cries against an exaggerated Negro menace which maintained party orthodoxy and justified cheating in elections. An entire generation had been told they must endure patiently or suffer at the hands of the Negro. These white people now felt, with understandable though perverse logic, that subordination of the Negro would be essential to a recovery of freedom and independence for themselves.

In 1906 the distressed white people of Georgia at last staged a successful political revolution in the state. Tom Watson, the frustrated and embittered farm leader of the 1890's, returned to politics and promised to support the election of any candidate who would pledge to disfranchise the Negro. The Negroes became the central issue of the campaign, attacked as brutes, rapists, criminals: by rejecting the Negro, the people would be rejecting the politics and economics of the New South industrialists who had dominated state government since Reconstruction. Hoke Smith, representative of the common people, defeated Clark Howell, publisher of the Atlanta *Constitution* and representative of the state's business leaders, for governor. Smith's election was viewed at the time as a celebration of the people's freedom from corporation rule, and Smith's platform included true Progressive reforms. But during the election, the Atlanta newspapers had featured inflammatory attacks against the Negroes, as criminals unfit for citizenship; as a tragic sequel to the election, Atlanta exploded in a four-day race riot in September, 1906, during which a mob of five thousand people killed ten Negroes and two whites, wounded sixty blacks and ten whites. Smith had pledged to disfranchise the Negro, and this was done in 1908 by constitutional amendment, making Georgia the sev-

The Atlanta riot of 1906, on the front page of a French newspaper. *Atlanta Historical Society*

enth state to disfranchise the Negro. To vote, a person would have to be a Confederate veteran or descended from one, a person of good character and citizenship, a person who could read and write any part of the U. S. or Georgia constitutions, or the owner of forty acres of land or property worth $500, with all poll taxes paid back to 1877.

The revival of the Ku Klux Klan at Atlanta in 1915 was further evidence of Georgia's social distress. For the Klan offered a mystical world of knight-hawks, ghouls, king kleagles, klaliffs, klokards, kludds, klabels, kladds, klorogoes, and klexters, the thrill of power and an illusion of importance to frustrated and impotent white people who had been unable to shape their own secure place in the world for nearly two generations since the Civil War. Patrollers of whites had scouted the plantation districts of the South before the Civil War to keep an eye on the slaves, and during Reconstruction a Klan had regulated the conduct of freedmen between 1867 and 1869, visiting the houses of idle or troublesome blacks, terrifying them with ghostly scenes, whipping them into subordination and warning them of future visits. Sporadic floggings of Negroes had been common during the late nineteenth century across the Georgia countryside. In 1915 William Simmons, a sometime Alabama minister and salesman, claimed that he was reviving the old Klan. But the new organization was a busy fraternal order with elaborate paraphernalia, gimmickry, rituals. Negro proscriptions were only part of a dogma which included attacks on Catholics, Jews and foreigners, a reaction to great national changes—the world war, rising tides of immigration from central Europe, shifting patterns of industry and cities—many of the same impulses which had created, more positively, the Progressive movement. The new Klan was stronger in Texas, Oklahoma and Arkansas than in the states of the Old South, most of whose major urban daily newspapers kept up a running attack on it. The Klan was perhaps more of a curi-

The Ku Klux Klan, revived at Atlanta in 1915, offered a thrill of power to frustrated white people. Jones County in the 1950's. *AP/Wide World Photos*

osity than a powerful force, but nevertheless it was a threatening statement of social distress.

Another wild symptom of the frustrations of Georgia people was the dramatic rise of lynchings after the 1890's, a development which paralleled the collapse of the cotton economy and the political disappointments of radical reform by the Populists. Scholars have shown a direct relationship between the per acre value of cotton and the number of lynchings in nine cotton states of the South between 1900 and 1930: when the price of cotton was high, the lynchings were few; when the price was low, the lynchings increased. The Panic of 1893, when cotton prices declined to less than five cents a pound, below the cost of production, was followed by the political debacle of 1894, with violent results. Between 1889 and 1918 Georgians lynched at least 386 people —more than any other state—of whom 360 were Negroes. In the dullness and insecurity of rural Southern life, frustrated people were lashing out spastically, desperately against the weakest people in their local neighborhoods, the Negroes on whom they were blaming their political frustrations and whose material progress threatened their place in society. In 1921, Governor Hugh M. Dorsey published a list of 135 examples of alleged mistreatment of Negroes in Georgia during the preceding two years, which included lynchings, peonage, floggings, cruelty. "In some counties," the governor reported, "the negro is being driven out as though he were a wild beast. In others he is being held as a slave. In others, no negroes remain."

As the distressed poor whites and blacks moved into Georgia cities after 1900 from their impoverished farms, these cities began to pass municipal ordinances against blacks. Augusta was the first city to segregate its street cars in 1900. Canton, population 847, allowed no Negroes except nurses to enjoy the public park in 1906. Savannah did not establish segregated streetcars until 1906, though such laws had

Lynching of Lint Shaw, Royston, 1936.
AP/Wide World Photos

been proposed earlier. In 1905 the Southern Bank of Savannah began labelling its teller windows by race, and in 1906 Ray Stannard Baker found elevators in Atlanta marked: "This car for Colored Passengers, Freight, Express and Packages." Atlanta, billed by its promoters as a liberal national city, enacted more segregation laws than any other Georgia town, because its population was large and more fluid, composed of displaced whites who resented the urban blacks who had been freed from the traditional social patterns of their rural communities. In 1925 Negro barbers in Atlanta were forbidden to serve white women and children. In 1931 it became illegal for a member of one race to move into a house previously occupied by a member of the other race, when the house was within fifteen blocks of a public school. In 1942 Albany required separate ticket booths and waiting lines for whites and blacks at theaters. In 1932 it was illegal for amateur sports teams of one race to play within two blocks of a playground set aside for members of the other race, in Atlanta. In 1940 Atlanta's parks were all segregated, except for the city zoo. In 1945 Atlanta officially segregated all theaters, arenas and public halls. Segregation, a relatively recent development, paralleled the final collapse of the South's agricultural empire and the movement of displaced whites and blacks into Southern cities. The system became so complete that white Southerners practically never saw Negroes except in formalized circumstances, since they were excluded from most places of amusement for whites and from most employment except agriculture and personal service. Blacks moved into a separate world, which included separate Bibles for court swearings, side entrances to railroad stations and separate waiting rooms, having to sit at the back of buses, stand at the end of lunch counters or at the kitchen entrance, watch a movie only in a Negro theater or from the second balcony of a white one.

In 1948, Lillian Smith, an ardent feminist and defender of civil rights in Georgia, recalled her Southern childhood: "I can almost touch

Segregated water fountains, Georgia, the 1950's.
Elliott Erwitt (top), Danny Lyon (bottom), Magnum Photos

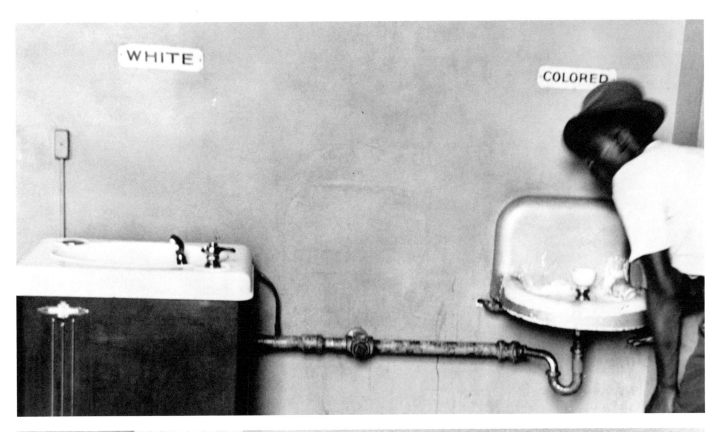

Black school, Greene County, 1941.
Jack Delano, Library of Congress

that little town, a little white town rimmed with Negroes. There it lies, broken in two by a strange idea, segregation. There are signs everywhere. White . . . colored . . . white . . . colored . . . over doors of railroad and bus stations, over doors of public toilets, over doors of theaters, over drinking fountains. There are signs without words: big white church, little unpainted colored church, big white school, little ramshackly colored school, big white house, little unpainted cabins; white graveyard with marble shafts, colored graveyards with mounds of dirt. There are the invisible lines: places you go, places you don't go; white town, colored town; white streets, colored streets; front door, back door; places you sit, places you cannot sit. Little Southern children learn their ritual." However accurate in part, impressions became stereotypes that became prejudices; however understandable historically, customs became rules that became rigid segregation.

Since all Georgians were poor, blacks tended to receive less than their separate but equal share of education. Until January, 1961, no Negro had ever attended a white school or college in Georgia. In Columbus in 1877–78, the school system enrolled 1,485 whites and 1,387 Negroes: the whites received $7,219 for teacher salaries, the blacks $1,530 for teacher salaries; the whites received $147.30 for heating fuel, the blacks $36. In 1874, Macon had 492 whites and 400 blacks in schools: there were six white schools and one black school, fourteen white teachers and eight Negro teachers. In 1900 Athens had the only high school for Negroes in all of the state of Georgia. In 1901 Jefferson County reported 1,703 whites and 2,036 Negroes in its schools, with forty-six white teachers and thirty Negro teachers. In 1906 the Georgia Equal Rights Commission proclaimed that of every one dollar of state school funds, only twenty cents was spent for Negro education. In all Georgia in 1926, only 1.9 percent of the black schools were made of brick or stone; sixty percent of the Negro schools were rented, compared with only twenty-one percent of the white schools;

78.5 percent of Negro schools were one-room buildings, compared with 32.8 percent for the whites. In 1930 the state of Georgia expended for each white child in school $35.42, but only $6.38 for each black child. In 1937–38 Negro teachers, principals and supervisors were paid $352, while white employees were paid $876.

In September, 1936, J. A. Lee of Albany wrote to Mrs. Franklin D. Roosevelt in the White House about the inequality of schools in Albany: "The population is equally divided between white and colored. Seventeen hundred colored pupils were enrolled during the school year 1935–36, but this number could not be accommodated on account of inadequate buildings. The school buildings for colored children are three frame buildings, aged, in need of repair, one condemned by [the] building inspector, another a temporary structure formerly used for housing tools during the construction of a $250,000 white high school. The white buildings are four elementary and two high schools, all brick or stucco. Funds have been used in improving playgrounds for white children, constructing a large football stadium. . . . Nothing as yet has been done to relieve the inadequate facilities for colored schools. Progress in education will be impeded as long as such conditions exist."

Disfranchisement closed the door of hope to half of Georgia's people, for inevitably the whole system of public service, government and justice would become unresponsive to the needs of people who could not vote. In law, Negroes tended to be more harshly punished than whites, for they did not generally serve on juries. In the aftermath of the Civil War, Georgia decided to lease its convicts to private work camps instead of building new prisons. John B. Gordon and Joseph E. Brown, two leading industrialists of that era, leased large numbers of convicts to work in their mines, lumber camps and brickyards. Most of these chain gang prisoners were Negroes: in 1873, there were 524 blacks and 90 whites in Georgia's chain gangs; in 1894, 2,137 blacks

Chain gang, Hood's Chapel, August, 1936.
Margaret Bourke-White from You Have Seen Their Faces *(New York, 1937) with permission*

Black convicts and white guard, Oglethorpe County, 1941.
Jack Delano, Library of Congress

and 191 whites; in 1911, 2,167 blacks and 180 whites. Vagrancy laws, contract labor laws, lien laws surrounded and encumbered the indebted, uneducated freedmen and their descendants. In 1911 W. J. Northen, former governor of Georgia, proposed with sincerely good intentions that the state "confine at some helpful service" all idle, incorrigible and vicious Negroes and keep them "until they become fit to put upon the community again." At worst, a confused Negro might work himself deep into debt as a sharecropper; then, realizing that he was only getting more indebted each year, he might try to run away from his landlord; the landlord would then have him arrested for evading his debts and then pay him out of jail, with the court compelling the Negro to continue working for his landlord; the landlord might even offer to "sell" the indebted Negro to another white man. A different code of justice for Negroes had evolved. Sporadic floggings of Negroes in rural Georgia continued at least until the late 1940's.

These disadvantages, closing the doors for advancement, tended to make blacks more and more into what many whites had always believed—ignorant, childlike, shiftless, immoral, criminal and unfit for full citizenship. In 1947 Katherine Lumpkin recalled the petty and profound injustices unthinkingly inflicted: "We knew the streets were the white man's wherever he chose to walk, that a Negro who moved out into the gutter to let us pass was in our eyes a 'good darkie.' I could have been hardly more than eight when a little Negro girl of our age, passing a friend and me, did not give ground. Her arm brushed against my companion's. She turned on the Negro child furiously. We were whites! 'Move over there, you dirty black nigger!' We often spoke of the peculiar inborn traits of this so peculiar race. White men stole, but not 'as a race.' We believed that a Negro could not help but steal. In their mental development none could ever go beyond, say, a child of ten or twelve. We used phrases such as 'thieving propensities,' 'innately irresponsible,' 'love of finery,' 'not to be trusted' and a dozen more."

Arthur Raper, a North Carolina-born social worker who went to Putnam County in 1934, was run out of Eatonton by whites angered at the arrival of his black assistants who were educated, well-clothed, addressed by titles and employed by the Federal government: "Many white farmers and mill workers were disturbed over seeing these prosperous, strange Negroes in good cars when so many whites were hard up and on relief. A drunk man announced that he didn't like 'dressed-up niggers' being here. It didn't make any difference how well trained they were, the white people needed the jobs. 'Do you mean to tell me that any nigger, however much education he has, can do a better job than a white man can do, even if he didn't have no training?'" Lillian Smith recalled: "Little Southern children learn their ritual. Some, if their faces are dark, learn to bend, hat in hand; others, if their faces are white, learn to hold their heads high. Some bending, genuflecting, giving in, some shoving, ignoring, demanding, avoiding. Children moving through a labyrinth made by grownups' greed and guilt and fear. . . . These ceremonials, performed from babyhood, slip from the conscious mind and become difficult to tear out." Thus, segregation, and the discrimination and neglect that followed in its wake, though a relatively recent development from the 1890's, was woven into the fabric of Southern life.

Tom Watson had predicted in 1907: "The great mass of negroes would gradually reconcile themselves to the condition of a recognized peasantry—a laboring class—within whose reach, as human beings, is every essential of happiness. The negro politician would migrate, the over-educated negro gravitate to the other side of Mason and Dixon's line; the more ambitious and restless of the race would leave the South. Those of the negroes who would remain, would know upon what terms they did so; would occupy the position of laborers simply; and thus the negro would cease to be a peril." One afternoon a white

Henry Mitchell wearing shoes made of old automobile
tires, Greene County, 1941. *Jack Delano, Library of
Congress*

Child selling "Baits such is miners, crickets, roches, tarket worms," Augusta, 1936. *Margaret Bourke-White from You Have Seen Their Faces (New York, 1937) with permission*

merchant in Albany scolded a black customer: "Why, you niggers have an easier time than I do!" To which the Negro replied: "Yes, and so does yo' hogs."

During the Depression, the American government became committed to the idea of using the State as an instrument of social change. The Southern states, too poor to reject Federal relief even with guidelines attached, became channels for this social legislation and for new governmental services which were the permanent outgrowth of relief. During World War II, America and "the democracies" had asserted a worldwide moral leadership, and, during the subsequent Cold War, the United States had to demonstrate to the world how all of its citizens were free and possessed equal opportunities for life and the pursuit of happines. Since World War I, significant numbers of Negroes had migrated from the South; during the 1940's alone, the number of blacks living outside the South jumped from 2,360,000 to 4,600,000. And so the South's peculiar problem became a national one, to which Northern politicians were now responsive.

In the South, other forces were also at work reviving the people who lived in the region's quiet countryside. The final collapse of cotton planting, ending an agricultural system dating back to Eli Whitney's invention of the cotton gin, was perhaps the most important factor in Georgia's future social and economic progress. In 1930, 3,426,000 acres of cotton were harvested in Georgia, but in 1970 only 380,000 acres were harvested. The migration of Negroes away from Georgia altered the composition of the society and reduced the potential threat which whites might feel toward them: in 1890 Negroes made up 47 percent of Georgia's population; in 1930, they were 37 percent; in 1960, 29 percent; in 1970, only 26.1 percent. During the Depression, whites at last abandoned their ruined farms and that traditional, slow-moving world and migrated to busy, progressive cities. The number of farm tenant operators in Georgia declined from a high 62.8 percent in 1930 to 9.2 percent of the farm population in 1969. Cotton had been eliminated as the dominant source of Southern wealth, and one machine could now do the work of eighty men; with these developments there was no longer an economic need to maintain a cheap labor supply, to keep the Negro in his place. During World War II and immediately afterwards, industrialization had really come to the South. During the decade 1940–1950, the South's industrial capacity grew 40 percent and its urban population increased 35.9 percent. As the Atlanta *Constitution* prophesied correctly in December, 1945: "When the history of this time is written some thirty to fifty years from now, it is likely that the first postwar years will be recorded as the years in which the South made its greatest strides toward a way of living that balanced agriculture with industry." In 1950 there were 3,800,000 farm jobs and 2,400,000 manufacturing jobs in the South; in 1972, there were 1,500,000 farm jobs and 4,400,000 factory jobs in the region. Georgia per capita income, which had been $340 in 1932, was $3,332 in 1970. Median income, which had been $1,902 in 1949, was $4,208 in 1959. The median years of schooling completed by Georgians twenty-five years or older increased from 7.8 years in 1950 to 10.8 years in 1970. In 1910 only 20.6 percent of Georgia was "urban," compared with 55.3 percent in 1960 and 60 percent in 1970. In short, each year Georgians were becoming more white, more urban, more industrialized, more educated, "more American."

Meanwhile, the Depression and World War II had given Southerners, isolated by the Civil War, an opportunity to enlist in two great national crusades. Hundreds of thousands of Southerners had expanded their horizons during the war years. Radio and television broke down the isolation of rural life, a process begun a half century earlier by rural free mail delivery and rural electrification. A new

Display window of commercial photographer, Savannah, 1936
Walker Evans, Library of Congress

generation was growing up in the South. Both Roosevelt and Eisen-hower, national heroes of the Depression and World War II, were personally beloved in Georgia, where they spent much time, Roosevelt at Warm Springs and Eisenhower at Augusta and Thomasville. During the 1950's, Georgians were chairman of the Senate Foreign Relations Committee, president of the World Bank, president of the Rockefeller Foundation, winner of a Pulitzer prize, president of the American Bar Association. In 1945 the Georgia legislature, prodded by liberal Governor Ellis Arnall, eliminated the poll tax and all other qualifications for voting, and in 1946 the Supreme Court upheld the right of Negroes to vote in white primaries. So in April, 1946, Georgia became the first state in the Deep South to have neither a poll tax nor a white primary. Some 100,000 Negroes voted in 1946. By 1952, 23.3 percent of Georgia blacks were registered to vote; by 1960, 29.3 percent were registered; by 1966, 44.4 percent were registered; by 1970, 64.4 percent were registered. The last surviving Confederate veteran died in Texas in 1959.

Between World War II and the early 1950's the Supreme Court asserted its authority to equalize civil rights, without confronting the specific, significant issue of school desegregation. In June, 1944, the Court ruled that a state could not require segregation of white and Negro passengers on buses and trains which crossed state lines. In February, 1948, President Truman proposed a ten-point civil rights program, including legislation against lynching, the poll tax and Jim Crow laws in interstate commerce, and creation of a fair employment practices commission and a commission on civil rights. In May, 1948, the Court ruled that no persons who purchased or rented property could be bound by restrictive covenants designed to exclude Negroes. In July, 1948, President Truman ordered fair employment practices throughout the federal government, including desegregation of the armed forces. In June, 1950, the Supreme Court ruled in three separate decisions that segregated Pullman dining cars violated the Interstate

Assembling airplanes, Warner Robins, 1943.
Library of Congress

Commerce Act, that the University of Texas should admit a Negro to its law school and that the University of Oklahoma should admit a Negro to fully integrated class life.

Ellis Arnall, governor of Georgia 1943–46 and the youngest governor in the United States at the time, was a rare progressive voice in the South and the only prominent public official in Georgia to defend Negro rights until after 1960. He prodded the state legislature to revise the state constitution, eliminating restrictions on Negro voting. Whether because of conviction or expediency, all prominent politicians in Georgia between 1946 and 1960 condemned the Supreme Court and the Negro. In 1946 former Governor Eugene Talmadge ran for governor, campaigning for the preservation of the white primary, which had been outlawed by the Court in April, 1946. When the Supreme Court ruled that states could not enforce segregation on interstate commerce, Talmadge proposed maintaining Jim Crow in Georgia by requiring passengers to purchase new tickets as they entered the state. In 1948, when Eugene Talmadge's son Herman was campaigning for governor, he vowed to uphold states' rights and obstruct FEPC legislation which had been proposed by President Truman. During the 1948 and 1950 campaigns, Herman Talmadge promised to preserve segregation.

In May, 1954, the Supreme Court ruled that separate schools were inherently unequal and directed that where school segregation existed —in seventeen states, the Old South, some border states, Oklahoma, Delaware and Missouri—it must end. In November, 1955, the Court ruled that segregation was illegal in public parks, playgrounds and golf courses. In late 1955, Negroes in Montgomery, Alabama, boycotted public buses, trying to end segregation on the local transit system. In December, Atlanta's white golf courses, but not pools and playgrounds, were opened to Negroes. In April, 1956, the Court ruled in a South Carolina case that segregation in intrastate transportation

Assembling cardboard boxes, Union Point, 1941
Library of Congress

was also unconstitutional. In November, 1956, the Court ruled that an Alabama law and Montgomery city ordinance segregating buses were illegal. In January, 1957, a group of Negro ministers in Atlanta was arrested trying to desegregate city buses. In September, 1957, over objections from the Arkansas governor, a federal judge ruled that immediate desegregation of Little Rock schools would have to proceed, and President Eisenhower sent U. S. troops to back up that order. In September, 1958, after plans had been drawn to lease Little Rock's public schools as "private schools," the Supreme Court ruled that such evasive schemes could not nullify the Court's desegregation instructions. In Arkansas, the President and Court had demonstrated in 1958 their determination to enforce desegregation. By December, 1958, suits had been filed in Atlanta against segregation of city buses and schools, in the local state college, at the restaurant of the city airport, but, although five years had passed since the original Court ruling, no desegregation had taken place in Georgia. In June, the U. S. district court at Atlanta ordered the school board to cease segregation and present a plan for desegregation. In August, 1959, integration of Little Rock schools took place. In December, the Atlanta board of education prepared a desegregation plan and submitted it to the district judge, who accepted the proposal with minor changes.

In the fall of 1954, Marvin Griffin had been elected governor, proclaiming, "Come hell or high water, races will not be mixed in Georgia schools!" In November, a constitutional amendment was passed which gave the governor and legislature the power to abolish the public schools and create a system of private schools. In September, 1955, Herman Talmadge and Governor Griffin helped organize a states' rights council of Georgia, loosely affiliated with white citizens' councils in other states, to preserve segregation. In December, Governor Griffin attempted to order the University of Georgia's board of regents, its governing trustees, to prohibit any state college from

Making socks, Union Point, 1941.
Library of Congress

playing with a nonsegregated sports team or before a nonsegregated audience. In April, 1956, the state parks director announced that nine Georgia parks would be leased to private citizens to perpetuate segregation. In April, the Georgia attorney general said he would recommend enactment of laws making it a capital crime for any public official in Georgia to enforce the U. S. desegregation rulings. When Negroes began to apply to white colleges in the late 1950's, the board of regents tightened entrance requirements to keep them out, and Southern governors agreed to finance regional graduate schools for Negroes so they would not enter state schools. In February, 1957, Senator Talmadge introduced legislation in Congress to deny federal courts jurisdiction over school integration cases. In January, 1958, Governor Griffin promised to close Atlanta's public schools rather than integrate them. When Ernest Vandiver was sworn in as governor in January, 1958, he pledged to preserve segregation, and in July he hired a special team of lawyers to figure how to do it. In 1960 Herman Talmadge spoke for six hours in the U. S. Senate—the longest speech of his senatorial career—against civil rights.

So in the spring of 1960 Georgia faced a critical choice: accept the rulings of the federal court to desegregate Georgia schools or close them. In February, 1960, the general assembly created a school study commission which toured ten cities in each congressional district to learn the people's feelings about the issue. While politicians wanted defiance, moderate and pragmatic business and professional men spoke out for compliance. The president of the Georgia Bar Association publicly urged the repeal of segregation laws. In April the commission made the momentous decision to recommend keeping Georgia's schools open. In 1961 the first integration of Georgia schools took place, when two students entered the University of Georgia at Athens and eight Negroes entered four Atlanta public schools. In 1962, pressed by court action, boycotts, demonstrations and an ICC

Police struggling with anti-segregation demonstrators, Atlanta, c. 1963. *Danny Lyon, Magnum Photos*

ruling, all segregated travel facilities in Georgia were ended, and the four major cities desegregated their bus systems.

In 1961, Ivan Allen, a progressive businessman, was elected mayor of Atlanta, defeating Lester Maddox, reactionary segregationist. In 1962, the U.S. District Court enjoined Georgia's Democrat party from using the county unit system, ending an anachronism that had allowed rural legislators to dominate city voters for fifty years. In the same year, a strident segregationist, Marvin Griffin, who appealed to the lingering prejudices of rural voters, was defeated for governor by a self-proclaimed moderate, Carl Sanders, who appealed to city voters. In 1963, Martin Luther King, Jr., the black minister from Atlanta who became arguably the most influential Georgian who ever lived, proclaimed on the steps of the Lincoln Memorial at Washington: "I have a dream, I have a dream that one day on the red hills of Georgia the sons of former slaves and the sons of former slaveowners will be able to sit down together at the table of brotherhood." In 1963 LeRoy Johnson became the first black state senator in ninety-two years, and the galleries of the Georgia Capitol were desegregated. That industrialization and economic expansion coincided with the civil rights movement helped insure its success. During the decade 1960–70, for the first time since the Civil War more people moved into the Southern states than left them. In the decade 1980–90, for the first time since the exodus of blacks to Northern cities began about 1900, their descendants began returning to the South. And so the people of Georgia entered a new era of progress and opportunity, which became possible only when they broke the continuity and abandoned the traditions of their agrarian past.

Martin Luther King, Jr., with his wife, at the Atlanta airport, on his way to Alabama to serve a five-day jail sentence for anti-segregation protests, 1967. *UPI/Bettmann*

GEORGIA

Bibliography

This selected list of materials—monographs, articles and published documents—has been arranged chronologically by subject. It is intended as a guide to further reading and also as an acknowledgement to other writers in the absence of footnotes. The reader is reminded that this bibliography was prepared in 1975 and does not include publications of the last seventeen years. Abbreviations: *GHQ* (*Georgia Historical Quarterly*); *MVHR* (*Mississippi Valley Historical Review*); *JSH* (*Journal of Southern History*); *GR* (*Georgia Review*); *GHS* (*Georgia Historical Society*).

I. COLONY, 1733–82

1. Studies and Articles

W. B. Stevens, *The History of Georgia* [1859], Savannah, 1972

Trevor R. Reese, *Colonial Georgia*, Athens, 1963

James R. McCain, *Georgia as a Proprietary Province*, Boston, 1917

Larry E. Ivers, *British Drums on the Southern Frontier, Military Colonization of Georgia, 1733–49*, Chapel Hill, 1974

Milton Ready, "An Economic History of Colonial Georgia, 1732–54," unpublished Ph.D. dissertation, University of Georgia, 1970

Verner W. Crane, "Promotional Literature of Georgia," in *Bibliographical Essays*, Cambridge, 1924

E. M. Coulter, "Was Georgia Settled by Debtors?," *GHQ*, LIII, 1969

H. B. Fant, "Picturesque Thomas Coram, Projector of Two Georgias and Father of the London Foundling Hospital," *GHQ*, XXXII, 1948

Kenneth Coleman, "The Southern Frontier, Georgia's Founding and the Expansion of South Carolina," *GHQ*, LVI, 1972

Kenneth Coleman, "Life in Oglethorpe's Georgia," *GR*, XVII, 1963

Trevor R. Reese, "Britain's Military Support of Georgia in the War of 1739–48," *GHQ*, XLIII, 1959

Randall M. Miller, "The Failure of the Colony of Georgia under the Trustees," *GHQ*, LIII, 1969

Percy Scott Flippin, "Royal Government in Georgia, 1752–76," *GHQ*, VII, 1924, et seq.

W. W. Abbot, *The Royal Governors of Georgia, 1754–75*, Chapel Hill, 1959

Jack P. Greene, "The Georgia Commons House of Assembly and the Power of Appointment to Executive Offices, 1765–75," *GHQ*, XLVI, 1962

C. Ashley Ellefson, "James Habersham and Georgia Loyalism, 1764–75," *GHQ*, XLIV, 1960

Randall M. Miller, "The Stamp Act in Georgia," *GHQ*, LVI, 1972

C. Ashley Ellefson, "The Stamp Act in Georgia," *GHQ*, XLVI, 1962

Spencer B. King, "Georgia and the American Revolution: Three Shades of Opinion," *GR*, XXIII, 1969

Kenneth Coleman, *The American Revolution in Georgia, 1763–89*, Athens, 1958

L. Van Loan Naiswald, "Major General Howe's Activities in South Carolina and Georgia, 1776–79," *GHQ*, XXXV, 1951

Patrick J. Furlong, "Civilian-Military Conflict and the Restoration of the Royal Province of Georgia, 1778–82," *JSH*, XXXVIII, 1972

Kenneth Coleman, "Restored Colonial Georgia, 1779–82," *GHQ*, XL, 1956

Alexander A. Lawrence, "James Jackson: Passionate Patriot," *GHQ*, XXXIV, 1950

Alexander A. Lawrence, *Storm over Savannah*, Athens, 1951

Robert S. Lambert, "The Flight of the Georgia Royalists," *GR*, XVII, 1963

2. Printed Sources

Mark Catesby, *The Natural History of Carolina, Florida and the Bahama Islands* [1731–51], Savannah, 1974

Trevor R. Reese, ed., *The Most Delightful Country of the Universe: Promotional Literature of the Colony of Georgia*, Savannah, 1972 [Contents: Mountgomery, *Discourse Concerning the design'd Establishment of a New Colony*, 1717; *A Description of the Golden Islands*, 1720; Jean Pierre Purry, *Memorial . . . to His Grace the Duke of Newcastle*, 1724; *Some Account of the Designs of the Trustees for establishing the Colony of Georgia*, 1732; *Select Tracts relating to Colonies*, 1732; James Oglethorpe, *A New and Accurate Account of the Provinces of South Carolina and Georgia*, 1732; Benjamin Martyn, *Reasons for Establishing the Colony of Georgia*, 1733; T. Rundle, *Sermon Preached . . . to recommend the Charity for establishing the New Colony of Georgia*, 1734]

E. M. Coulter, ed., "A List of the First Shipload of Georgia Settlers," *GHQ*, XXXI, 1947

E. M. Coulter and A. B. Saye, eds., *A List of the Early Settlers of Georgia*, Athens, 1949

Robert G. McPherson, "The Voyage of the Anne, A Daily Record," *GHQ*, XLIV, 1960

Mills Lane, ed., *General Oglethorpe's Georgia, Colonial Letters 1733–43*, 2 vols., Savannah, 1975

"Letters from General Oglethorpe to the Trustees and Others 1735–44," in GHS *Collections*, III, Savannah, 1873

Allen D. Candler, comp., *Original Papers, 1734–52, Colonial Records of the State of Georgia*, XX, XXI, XXII, pts. 1 and 2, XXIII, XXIV, XXV, XXVI, XXXV, XXXVI; volumes XX, XXXV and XXXVI unpublished manuscripts; others Atlanta, 1910–16

Allen D. Candler, comp., "Letter Books of the Trustees 1732–52," CRSG, XXIX, XXX, XXXI, unpublished manuscripts, State Dept. of Archives and History, Atlanta

Trevor R. Reese, ed., *Our First Visit in America, Early Reports from the Colony of Georgia*, Savannah, 1974 [Contents: journals of Peter Gordon, 1732–35; Von Reck and Bolzius, 1734; Francis Moore, 1735; Benjamin Ingham, 1735–36; John Wesley, 1735–38; Thomas Causton, 1737; George Whitefield, 1738–40]

Trevor R. Reese, ed., *The Clamorous Malcontents, Criticisms and Defenses of the Colony of Georgia*, Savannah, 1973 [Contents: *A State of the Province of Georgia . . . 1740*; Patrick Tailfer, *A True and Historical Narrative of the Colony of Georgia*, 1741; Benjamin Martyn, *An Impartial Enquiry into the State and Utility of the Province of Georgia*, 1741; *An Account Shewing the Progress of the Colony of Georgia in America*, 1741; Thomas Stephens, *The Hard Case of the Distressed People of Georgia*, 1742; Thomas Stephens, *A Brief Account of the Causes that have retarded the Progress of the Colony of Georgia*, 1743]

William Stephens, *Journal of the Proceedings in Georgia* [1737–1740], I–III, London, 1743

E. M. Coulter, ed., *Journal of William Stephens, 1741–45*, I–II, Athens, 1958–59

Robert G. McPherson, ed., *Journal of the Earl of Egmont*, Athens, 1962

Allen D. Candler, comp., *Journal of the Earl of Egmont*, CRSG, V, Atlanta, 1908

Historical Manuscripts Commission, *Diary of Viscount Percival*, I–III, London, 1922–23

Allen D. Candler, comp., *Journal of the Trustees 1732–52*, CRSG, I, Atlanta, 1904

Allen D. Candler, comp., *The Minutes of the Common Council of Trustees 1732–52*, CRSG, II, Atlanta, 1904

Lilla M. Hawes, ed., "A Description of Whitefield's Bethesda" [1748], *GHQ*, XLV, 1961

George F. Jones, ed., *Henry Newman's Salzburger Letterbooks*, Athens, 1966

George F. Jones, ed., *Detailed Reports of the Salzburger Emigrants*, I– , Athens, 1968–

George F. Jones, ed., "Commissary Von Reck's Report on Georgia" [1734], *GHQ*, XLVII, 1963

George F. Jones, ed., "John Martin Bolzius Reports on Georgia in 1739," *GHQ*, XLVII, 1963

George F. Jones, ed., "The Secret Diary of Pastor Johann Martin Bolzius" [1736], *GHQ*, LIII, 1969

Lothar L. Tresp, tr., "August, 1748, in Georgia from the Diary of John Martin Bolzius," *GHQ*, XLVII, 1963

Robert G. McPherson, "The Mutiny of St. Andrews, 1738, A Letter," *GHQ*, XLVII, 1960

Patrick Sutherland, *An Account of the Late Invasion of Georgia*, London, 1742

The Spanish Official Account of the Attack on the Colony of Georgia, GHS Collections, VII, pt. III, Savannah, 1913

Report of the Committee Appointed to examine into the Proceedings of the People of Georgia, Charlestown, 1736

The Report of the Committee of Both Houses of Assembly of the Province of South-Carolina . . . on the Late Expedition against St. Augustine, London, 1743

Don Manuel de Montiano, *Letters Related to the Siege of St. Augustine*, 1740, GHS Collections, VII, pt. I, Savannah, 1909

Isaac Kimber, *A Relation of the Late Expedition Against St. Augustine under General Oglethorpe*, London, 1742

George Cadogan, *The Spanish Hireling Detected*, London, 1743

A Full Reply to Lieutenant Cadogan's Spanish Hireling, etc. and Lieutenant Mackay's Letter, London, 1743

Allen D. Candler, comp., *Proceedings of the President and Assistants, 1741–54*, CRSG, VI, Atlanta, 1906

Lilla M. Hawes, ed., "Proceedings of the President and Assistants 1749–51," *GHQ*, XXXV, 1951

W. W. Abbot, ed., *King George's Georgia, Letters of the Royal Governors of Georgia, 1754–82*, Savannah, in press

Allen D. Candler, comp., *Proceedings and Minutes of the Governor and Council, 1754–82*, CRSG, VII–XII, Atlanta, 1906–07

Allen D. Candler, comp., *Journal of the Commons House of Assembly, 1755–82*, CRSG, XIII–XV, Atlanta, 1907

Allen D. Candler, comp., *Journal of the Upper House of Assembly, 1755–74*, CRSG, XVI–XVII, Atlanta, 1907–08

William Logan, "Journal of a Journey to Georgia, 1745," *Pennsylvania Magazine of History and Biography*, January, 1912, et seq.

G. Taylor, *A Voyage to North America in 1768 and 1769*, Nottingham, 1771

Thomas Raspberry, *Letterbook 1758–61*, GHS Collections, XIII, Savannah, 1959

James Habersham, *Letters 1756–75*, GHS Collections, VI, Savannah, 1904

Joseph Clay, *Letters 1776–93*, GHS Collections, VIII, Savannah, 1913

Louis DeVorsey, ed., *DeBrahm's Report of the General Survey in the Southern District of North America* [1771], Columbia, 1971

John J. Zubly, *The Law of Liberty*, Philadelphia, 1775

Benjamin Kennedy, ed., *Muskets, Cannon Balls and Bombs: Nine Narratives of the Siege of Savannah, 1779*, Savannah, 1974

Proceedings of the First Provincial Congress, 1775, Proceedings of the Georgia Council of Safety, 1775–77, in GHS *Collections*, V, pt. 1, 1901

Order Book of Samuel Elbert, 1776–78, and *Letter Book of Samuel Elbert, 1785*, in GHS *Collections*, V, pt. 2, 1902

C. C. Jones, ed., *The Siege of Savannah in 1779*, Albany, 1874

An Account of the Siege of Savannah, 1779, from a British Source, in GHS *Collections*, V, pt. 1, 1901

Anthony Stokes, *Desultory Observations*, London, 1792

Anthony Stokes, *A View of the Constitution of the British Colonies*, London, 1783

Anthony Stokes, *A Narrative of the Official Conduct of Anthony Stokes*, London, 1784

Lilla M. Hawes, ed., "Papers of Lachlan McIntosh, 1774–99," *GHQ*, XII, 1957

Lilla M. Hawes, ed., "Minutes of the Executive Council and Other Documents, 1777," *GHQ*, XXXIII, 1949

Lilla M. Hawes, ed., "Some Papers of the Governor and Council of Georgia, 1780–81," *GHQ*, XLVI, 1962

II. FRONTIER, 1782–1835

1. Studies and Articles

James Etheridge Callaway, *The Early Settlement of Georgia*, Athens, 1948

E. M. Coulter, *Old Petersburg and the Broad River Valley of Georgia*, Athens, 1965

U. B. Phillips, *Georgia and States' Rights*, Washington, 1902

Henry T. Malone, *Cherokees of the Old South*, Athens, 1956

Kenneth Coleman, "Social Life in Georgia in the 1780's," *GR*, IX, 1955

C. Burton Adams, "Yale Influence on the Formation of the University of Georgia," *GHQ*, LI, 1967

George R. Lamplugh, "Farewell to the Revolution: Georgia in 1785," *GHQ*, LVI, 1972

Ralph C. Scott, "The Quaker Settlement of Wrightsborough, Georgia," *GHQ*, LVI, 1972

Homer Bast, "Creek Indian Affairs, 1775–78," *GHQ*, XXXIII, 1949

Randolph C. Downes, "Creek-American Relations, 1782–90," *GHQ*, XXI, 1937

J. Leitch Wright, Jr., "Creek-American Treaty of 1790," *GHQ*, LI, 1967

Randolph C. Downes, "Creek-American Relations, 1790–95," *JSH*, VIII, 1942

Richard K. Murdoch, "Elijah Clarke and Anglo-American Designs on East Florida, 1797–98," *GHQ*, XXXV, 1951

Doyle Mathis, "Chisholm v. Georgia: Background and Settlement," *Journal of American History*, LIV, 1967

Henry T. Malone, "The Cherokee Phoenix: Supreme Expression of Cherokee Nationalism," *GHQ*, XXXIV, 1956

Henry Prentice Miller, "Significance and Background of Major Jones's Courtship," *GHQ*, XXX, 1946

U. B. Phillips, "Historical Notes on Milledgeville, Georgia," *Gulf States Historical Magazine*, II, 1903

Albert B. Saye, ed., "Journal of the Georgia Constitutional Convention of 1798," *GHQ*, XXXVI, 1952

John Bartram, *Diary of a Journey through the Carolinas, Georgia and Florida* [1765–66], Philadelphia, 1942

William Bartram, *Travels to North and South Carolina, Georgia, East and West Florida* [1773–77], Savannah, 1973

Mills Lane, ed., *The Rambler in Georgia*, Savannah, 1973 [Contents: Georgia travel accounts by La Rouchefoucauld-Liancourt, 1796; John Melish, 1806–09; John Lambert, 1808; Adam Hodgson, 1820; Basil Hall, 1828; James Stuart, 1830; C. D. Arfwedson, 1833; Tyrone Power, 1834; George Featherstonhaugh, 1836; James Silk Buckingham, 1839; George Lewis, 1844; Charles Lyell, 1845–46; Frederick Law Olmsted, 1853–54]

G. Melvin Herndon, "Samuel Edward Butler of Virginia Goes to Georgia, 1784," *GHQ*, LII, 1968

G. Melvin Herndon, ed., "The Diary of Samuel Edward Butler, 1784–86," *GHQ*, LII, 1968

Lilla M. Hawes, ed., "Miscellaneous Papers of James Jackson, 1781–98," *GHQ*, XXXVII, 1953

Lilla M. Hawes, ed., "Papers of James Jackson, 1781–98," *GHQ*, XXXVIII, 1954

Lilla M. Hawes, ed., "The Letter Book of General James Jackson, 1788–96," *GHQ*, XXXVII, 1953

John K. Mahon, ed., "Correspondence between General James Jackson and Captain William Ross," *GHQ*, XXXV, 1951

Harriet Milledge Salley, ed., *Correspondence of John Milledge* [1785–1818], Columbia, 1949

Marion A. Boggs, ed., *The Alexander Letters*, Savannah, 1916

Louis Milfort, *Memoirs, or My Sojourn in the Creek Nation* [1802], Savannah, 1972

Lilla M. Hawes, ed., "The Frontiers of Georgia in the Late 18th Century: Jonas Fauche to Joseph Vallance Bevan," *GHQ*, XLVII, 1963

Benjamin Hawkins, *Letters 1796–1806*, GHS *Collections*, IX, 1916

Benjamin Hawkins, *Sketch of the Creek Country in 1791–99*, GHS *Collections*, III, pt. II, 1848

Marion Hemperley, ed., "Benjamin Hawkins' Trip across Georgia in 1796," *GHQ*, LV, 1971

Marion Hemperley, ed., "Benjamin Hawkins' Trip across Western and Northern Georgia" [1798], *GHQ*, LVI, 1972

John Davis, *Travels of Four Years and a Half in the United States of America* [1799], London, 1803

Virginia Steele Wood and Ralph Van Wood, eds., "The Reuben King Journal, 1800–06," *GHQ*, L, 1966

Elmer T. Clark, ed., *Journal and Letters of Francis Asbury*, London, 1958

Raymond A. Mohl, ed., "A Scotsman Visits Georgia in 1811," *GHQ*, LV, 1971

Sidney Walter Martin, ed., "A New Englander's Impressions of Georgia in 1817–18: Extracts from the Diary of Ebenezer Kellogg," *JSH*, XII, 1946

Charlotte Newton, ed., "Ebenezer Newton's 1818 Diary," *GHQ*, LIII, 1969

William B. Hesseltine and Larry Gara, eds., "Across Georgia and into Alabama, 1817–18," *GHQ*, XXXVII, 1953

James C. Bonner, ed., "Journal of a Mission to Georgia in 1827," *GHQ*, XLIV, 1960

Achille Murat, *The United States of North America* [1826], London, 1833

John Hammond Moore, ed., "Jared Sparks in Georgia, April, 1826," *GHQ*, XLVII, 1963

Una Pope-Hennessy, *The Aristocratic Journey* [1828], New York, 1931

T. Conn Bryan, ed., "Letters concerning Georgia Gold Mines, 1830–34," *GHQ*, XLIV, 1960

James W. Covington, ed., "Letters from the Georgia Gold Region," *GHQ*, XXXIX, 1955

John H. Goddard, ed., "Some Letters of James Eppinger, 1832–46," *GHQ*, XLVII, 1964

John C. Dann, ed., "A Northern Traveller in Georgia, 1843," *GHQ*, LVI, 1972

T. A. Burke, ed., *Polly Peablossom's Wedding and Other Tales*, Philadelphia, 1851

A. B. Longstreet, *Georgia Scenes* [1835], Savannah, 1975

W. T. Thompson, *Major Jones's Courtship*, New York, 1883

William Malcolm Johnston, *Dukesborough Tales*, Madison, 1843

Adiel Sherwood, *A Gazeteer of the State of Georgia*, Washington, 1837

Thomas S. Woodward, *Reminiscences of the Creek or Muscogee Indians*, Birmingham, 1939

James S. Lamar, *Recollections of Pioneer Days in Georgia*, Washington, 1916

Garnett Andrews, *Reminiscences of an Old Georgia Lawyer*, Atlanta, 1870

Rebecca Latimer Felton, *Country Life in Georgia in the Days of My Youth*, Atlanta, 1919

George Gilmer, *Sketches of Some of the First Settlers of Upper Georgia*, New York, 1855

Wilson Lumpkin, *The Removal of the Cherokee Indians from Georgia*, New York, 1907

Stephen F. Miller, *The Bench and Bar of Georgia*, Philadelphia, 1858

Charles J. Latrobe, *The Rambler in North America* [1833], London, 1835

III. PLANTATIONS AND SLAVERY, 1835–60

1. Studies and Articles

Ralph B. Flanders, *Plantation Slavery in Georgia*, Chapel Hill, 1933

Ruth Scarborough, *The Opposition to Slavery in Georgia Prior to 1860*, Nashville, 1933

James C. Bonner, *A History of Georgia Agriculture, 1732–1860*, Athens, 1964

Richard H. Shryock, *Georgia and the Union in 1850*, Durham, 1926

E. M. Coulter, *College Life in the Old South*, Athens, 1951

Rudolph von Abele, *Alexander H. Stephens*, New York, 1946

Bertram Holland Flanders, *Early Georgia Magazines*, Athens, 1944

E. Merton Coulter, *Thomas Spalding of Sapelo*, University, 1940

John E. Simpson, "A Biography of Howell Cobb, 1815–61," unpublished Ph.D. dissertation, University of Georgia, 1971

Darold W. Wax, "Georgia and the Negro before the American Revolution," *GHQ*, LI, 1967

Betty Wood, "Thomas Stephens and the Introduction of Black Slavery in Georgia," *GHQ*, LVIII, 1974

U. B. Phillips, "Plantation as a Civilizing Factor," *Sewanee Review*, LII, 1904

E. M. Coulter, "A Century of a Georgia Plantation," *Mississippi Valley Historical Review*, XVI, 1929

William G. Proctor, "Slavery in Southwest Georgia," *GHQ*, XLIX, 1965

U. B. Phillips, "On the Economics of Slavery, 1815–60," *Annual Report of the American Historical Association*, Washington, 1912

U. B. Phillips, "Racial Problems, Adjustments, and Disturbances in the Ante-Bellum Period," in *The South in the Building of the Nation*, IV, Richmond, 1909

U. B. Phillips, "The Economic Cost of Slave-Holding in the Cotton Belt," *Political Science Quarterly*, XX, 1905

Thomas P. Govan, "Was Plantation Slavery Profitable?," *JSH*, VIII, 1942

James C. Bonner, "Genesis of Agricultural Reform in the Cotton Belt," *JSH*, IX, 1943

Thomas B. P. Govan, "Banking and the Credit System in Georgia, 1810–60," *JSH*, IV, 1938

Bowling C. Yates, "Macon, Georgia, Inland Trading Center, 1826–36," *GHQ*, LV, 1971

L. E. Roberts, "Educational Reform in Ante-Bellum Georgia," *GR*, XVI, 1962

R. P. Brooks, "Howell Cobb and the Crisis of 1850," *MVHR*, IV, 1917

2. Published Sources

U. B. Phillips, ed., *Plantation and Frontier Documents, 1649–1863*, Cleveland, 1909

James Ewell, *Planter's and Mariner's Medical Companion*, Philadelphia, 1807

Richard K. Murdoch, "Letters and Papers of Dr. Daniel Turner, 1804–08," *GHQ*, LIII, 1969, et seq.

John Livingston Hopkins, *Messalina's Questions; or, a Vindication of Slavery*, Liverpool, 1821

J. Jacobus Flournoy, *An Essay on the Origin, Habits, etc. of The African Race*, New York, 1835

William J. Hobby, *Remarks upon Slavery, occasioned by Attempts made to Circulate Improper Publications in the Southern States*, Philadelphia, 1835

Bondage a Moral Institution Sanctioned by the Scriptures by a Southern Farmer, Macon, 1837

Frances Anne Kemble, *Journal of a Residence on a Georgian Plantation* [1838–39], London, 1863

Emily P. Burke, *Reminiscences of Georgia* [1840–41], Oberlin, 1850

Slavery, A Treatise showing that Slavery is Neither a Moral, Political, nor Social Evil, Penfield, 1844

Moses Roper, *Narratives of the Adventure and Escape of Moses Roper from American Slavery*, Berwick-upon-Tweed, 1846

A. B. Longstreet, *A Voice from the South*, 1847

Samuel Dunwoody, *A Sermon upon the Subject of Slavery*, Marietta, 1850

Lewis W. Paine, *Six Years in a Georgia Prison*, New York, 1851

C. G. Memminger, *Lecture . . . Showing African Slavery to be Consistent with the Moral and Physical Progress of a Nation*, Augusta, 1851

Robert Toombs, *An Oration delivered before the Few and Phi Gamma Societies*, Augusta, 1853

Robert Collins, *Essay on the Treatment and Management of Slaves*, Boston, 1853

Charles Ball, *Slavery in the United States*, Pittsburgh, 1854

Nehemiah Adams, *A South-Side View of Slavery* [1854], Savannah, 1974

L. A. Chamerovzow, *Slave Life in Georgia* [1855], Savannah, 1972

William Grimes, *The Life of William Grimes, The Runaway Slave*, New Haven, 1855

Charles Grandison Parsons, *Inside View of Slavery* [1855], Savannah, 1974

Philo Tower, *Slavery Unmasked*, Rochester, 1856

John W. Park, *An Address on African Slavery*, Atlanta, 1857

Fifty Years in Chains or the Life of an American Slave, New York, 1858

Thomas R. R. Cobb, *An Historical Sketch of Slavery*, Philadelphia and Savannah, 1858

William Tappan Thompson, *The Slaveholder Abroad; or, Billy Buck's Visit with his Master to England*, Philadelphia, 1860

Marcus A. Bell, *Message of Love; South-Side View of Cotton is King; and the Philosophy of African Slavery*, Atlanta, 1860

E. N. Elliott, *Cotton is King and Pro-Slavery Arguments*, Augusta, 1860

Joseph R. Wilson, *Mutual Relation of Masters and Slaves as Taught in the Bible*, Augusta, 1861

Harrison Berry, *Slavery and Abolitionists as Viewed by a Georgia Slave*, Atlanta, 1861

E. W. Warren, *Nellie Norton; or, Southern Slavery and the Bible*, Macon, 1864

Ronald Killion and Charles T. Waller, *Slavery Time When I Was Chillun down on Marster's Plantation: Interviews with Georgia Slaves*, Savannah, 1973

C. A. L. Lamar, ed., "A Slave-Trader's Letter Book," *North American Review*, 143, 1886

Robert Manson Meyers, *Children of Pride*, New Haven, 1973

U. B. Phillips, ed., *Correspondence of Robert Toombs, Alexander H. Stephens and Howell Cobb*, Washington, 1913

R. Q. Mallard, *Plantation Days Before Emancipation*, Richmond, 1892

James Z. Rabun, ed., "Alexander H. Stephens's Diary, 1834–37," *GHQ*, XXXVI, 1952

IV. CIVIL WAR AND RECONSTRUCTION, 1861–72

1. Studies and Articles

T. Conn Bryan, *Confederate Georgia*, Athens, 1953

Michael P. Johnson, "A New Look at the Popular Vote for Delegates to the Georgia Secession Convention," *GHQ*, LVI, 1972

Ellen Louise Sumner, "Unionism in Georgia, 1860–61," unpublished M.A. thesis, University of Georgia, 1960

McWorter S. Cooley, "Manufacturing in Georgia during the Civil War Period," unpublished M.A. thesis, University of Georgia, 1929

Richard W. Griffin, "The Origins of the Industrial Revolution in Georgia: Cotton Textiles, 1810–65," *GHQ*, XLII, 1958

John F. Stover, "The Ruined Railroads of the Confederacy," *GHQ*, XLII, 1958

Alexander C. Niven, "Joseph E. Brown, Confederate Obstructionist," *GHQ*, XLII, 1958

Joseph H. Parks, "State Rights in a Crisis: Governor Joseph E. Brown versus President Jefferson Davis," *JSH*, XXXII, 1956

Virgil Sim Davis, "Stephen Elliott: A Southern Bishop in Peace and War," unpublished Ph.D. dissertation, University of Georgia, 1964

Earl Schenck Miers, *The General Who Marched to Hell*, New York, 1951

Ralph B. Singer, "Confederate Atlanta," unpublished Ph.D. dissertation, University of Georgia, 1973

James C. Bonner, "Sherman at Milledgeville in 1864," *JSH*, XXII, 1956

Robert C. Black III, "The Railroads of Georgia in the Confederate War Effort," *JSH*, XIII, 1947

James O. Breeden, "A Medical History of the Later Stages of the Atlanta Campaign," *JSH*, XXXV, 1969

C. Mildred Thompson, *Reconstruction in Georgia* [1915], Savannah, 1972

Alan Conway, *The Reconstruction of Georgia*, Minneapolis, 1966

2. Printed Sources

Richard B. Harwell, ed., "Louisiana Burge: The Diary of a Confederate College Girl," *GHQ*, XXXVI, 1952

Spencer B. King, ed., "Rebel Lawyer: The Letters of Lt. Theodore W. Montfort, 1861–62," *GHQ*, XLVIII, 1964

Charles H. Smith, *Bill Arp, so called, a Side Show of the Southern Side of the War*, New York, 1866

A. M. Cook, *Journal of a Milledgeville Girl, 1861–67*, Athens, 1964

Lilla M. Hawes, ed., "The Memoirs of Charles H. Olmstead," *GHQ*, XLII, 1958, et seq.

Willard E. Wight, ed., "The Diary of Rev. Charles S. Vedder, May–July, 1861," *GHQ*, XXXIX, 1955

T. Conn Bryan, "Letters of Two Confederate Officers: William Thomas Conn and Charles Augustus Conn," *GHQ*, XLVI, 1962

Benjamin Rountree, ed., "Letters from a Confederate Soldier," *GR*, XVIII, 1964

S. Joseph Lewis, Jr., ed., "Letters of William Fisher Plane to his Wife," *GHQ*, XLVIII, 1964

Edmund Cody Burnett, ed., "Letters of a Confederate Surgeon: Dr. Abner Embry McGarity, 1862–65," *GHQ*, XXIX, 1945, et seq.

William Irvine, "Diary and Letters of William N. White," *Atlanta Historical Bulletin*, X, 1937

Clyde C. Walton, *Private Smith's Journal*, Chicago, 1963

James M. Merrill, "Personne Goes to Georgia: Five Civil War Letters," *GHQ*, XLIII, 1959

Martin Abbott, ed., "Irrepressible Optimism of a Georgia Confederate Soldier in 1864: A Letter," *GHQ*, XXXVII, 1953

Andrew Forest Muir, ed., "The Battle of Atlanta as Described by a Confederate Soldier," *GHQ*, XLII, 1958

Charles Brockman, Jr., ed., "The John Van Duser Diary of Sherman's March from Atlanta to Hilton Head," *GHQ*, LIII, 1969

Donald W. Lewis, ed., "A Confederate Officer's Letters on Sherman's March to Atlanta," *GHQ*, LI, 1967

George W. Murray, *A History of George W. Murray and his Long Confinement at Andersonville, Georgia*, Northampton, 1865

Robert H. Kellogg, *Life and Death in Rebel Prisons*, Hartford, 1865

A. O. Abbott, *Prison Life in the South*, New York, 1865

Mills Lane, ed., *"War is Hell!" Sherman in Georgia*, Savannah, 1974

David P. Conyngham, *Sherman's March through the South*, New York, 1865

John H. Kennaway, *On Sherman's Track*, London, 1867

George Sharland, *Knapsack Notes of Sherman's Campaign through the State of Georgia*, Springfield, 1865

G. S. Bradley, *The Star Corps; or Notes of an Army Chaplain*, Milwaukee, 1865

George C. Osborn, "Sherman's March through Georgia: Letters from Charles Ewing to his Father, Thomas Ewing," *GHQ*, XLII, 1958

Henry Russell Hitchcock, *Marching through Georgia*, New Haven, 1927

James A. Padgett, "With Sherman through Georgia and the Carolinas: Letters of a Federal Soldier," *GHQ*, XXXII, 1948

"An Indiana Doctor Marches with Sherman," *Indiana Magazine of History*, XLIX, 1953

Oscar Osborn Winther, *With Sherman to the Sea*, Baton Rouge, 1943

Chauncey Cook, "Letters of a Badger Boy in Blue," *Wisconsin Magazine of History*, V, 1921–22

F. B. Joyner, "With Sherman in Georgia: A Letter from the Coast," *GHQ*, XLII, 1958

Wilfred W. Black, "Marching with Sherman through Georgia and the Carolinas," *GHQ*, LII, 1968

James I. Robertson, Jr., ed., *The Diary of Dolly Lunt Burge* [1917], Athens, 1962

Kate Cumming, *A Journal of the Hospital Life in the Confederate Army*, Nashville, 1866

T. Conn Bryan, ed., "A Georgia Woman's Civil War Diary: The Journal of Minerva Leah Rowles McClatchey, 1864–65," *GHQ*, LI, 1967

Eliza Frances Andrews, *The War-Time Journal of a Georgia Girl, 1864–65* [1908], Macon, 1960

Spencer B. King, Jr., ed., "Fanny Cohen's Journal of Sherman's Occupation of Savannah," *GHQ*, XLI, 1957

B. H. Hill, *Notes on the Situation*, Augusta, 1867

Adelaide L. Fries, "The Elizabeth Sterchi Letters," *Atlanta Historical Society Bulletin*, V, 1940

Whitelaw Reid, *After the War: A Southern Tour*, New York, 1866

Willard E. Wight, "Reconstruction in Georgia: Three Letters by Edwin G. Higbee," *GHQ*, XLI, 1957

John Richard Dennett, *The South as It Is* [1866], New York, 1965

J. T. Trowbridge, *The South*, Hartford, 1866

Carl Schurz, *Condition of the South*, Washington, 1866

Joseph E. Mahaffey, ed., "Carl Schurz's Letters from the South," *GHQ*, XXXV, 1951

William A. Campbell, ed., "A Freedman's Bureau Diary by George Wagner," *GHQ*, XLVIII, 1964

Sidney Andrews, *The South since the War*, Boston, 1970

J. W. Alvord, *Letters from the South Relating to the Condition of the Freedmen*, Washington, 1870

Robert Somers, *The Southern States Since the War*, New York, 1871

Charles Stearns, *The Black Man of the South and the Rebels*, New York, 1872

Charles Nordhoff, *The Cotton States in the Spring and Summer of 1875*, New York, 1876

David C. Barrow, Jr., "A Georgia Plantation," *Scribner's Magazine*, XXI, 1881

Frances Butler Leigh, *Ten Years on a Georgia Plantation Since the War*, London, 1883

V. THE NEW SOUTH, 1872–1908

1. Studies and Articles

R. B. Nixon, *Henry W. Grady: Spokesman of the New South*, New York, 1943

Paul M. Gaston, *The New South Creed*, New York, 1970

Broadus M. Mitchell, *The Rise of Cotton Mills in the South*, Baltimore, 1921

Willard Range, "Hannibal I. Kimball," *GHQ*, XXIX, 1945

Richard W. Griffin, "Problems of the Southern Cotton Planters after the Civil War," *GHQ*, XXXIX, 1955

Collamer M. Abbott, "New England Money Goes South," *GHQ*, XLIX, 1965

John F. Stover, "Northern Financial Interests in Southern Railroads, 1865–1900," *GHQ*, XXXIX, 1955

Enoch M. Banks, *The Economics of Land Tenure in Georgia*, New York, 1905

Charles S. Johnson, Edwin R. Embree, W. W. Alexander, *The Collapse of Cotton Tenancy*, Chapel Hill, 1935

Willard Range, *A Century of Georgia Agriculture, 1850–1950*, Athens, 1954

Arthur F. Raper, *Preface to Peasantry*, Chapel Hill, 1936

Rupert P. Vance, *Human Geography in the South*, Chapel Hill, 1935

Arthur F. Raper, *Tenants of the Almighty*, New York, 1943

T. J. Woofter, Jr., *Landlord and Tenant on the Cotton Plantation*, Washington, 1936

W. T. Couch, *Culture in the South*, Chapel Hill, 1934

Clarence Heer, *Income and Wages in the South*, Chapel Hill, 1930

Arthur F. Raper and Ira DeA. Reid, *Sharecroppers All*, Chapel Hill, 1941

Howard W. Odum, *Southern Regions of the United States*, Chapel Hill, 1936

J. B. Floyd, "Rebecca Latimer Felton, Political Independent," *GHQ*, xxx, 1946

Alex M. Arnett, *The Populist Movement in Georgia*, New York, 1922

Judson C. Ward, "The New Departure Democrats in Georgia: An Interpretation," *GHQ*, XLI, 1957

John E. Talmadge, "The Death Blow to Independentism in Georgia," *GHQ*, xxxIx, 1955

John E. Talmadge, *Rebecca Latimer Felton*, Athens, 1960

A. M. Arnett, "The Populist Movement in Georgia," *GHQ*, VII, 1923

C. Vann Woodward, *Tom Watson: Agrarian Rebel* [1938], Savannah, 1973

V. O. Key, Jr., *Southern Politics in State and Nation*, New York, 1949

Clarence Cason, *Ninety Degrees in the Shade*, Chapel Hill, 1935

Allen Lumpkin Henson, *Red Galluses*, Boston, 1945

Horace Montgomery, *Cracker Parties*, Baton Rouge, 1950

2. Printed Sources

Henry W. Grady, *The New South* [1880–89], Savannah, 1972

Atticus G. Haygood, *The New South*, Oxford, 1880

Albert V. House, Jr., ed., "A Reconstruction Sharecropper Contract on a Georgia Rice Plantation," *GHQ*, xxvi, 1942

W. D. Trammell, *Ça Ira*, New York, 1874

Thomas M. Norwood, *Plutocracy or American White Slavery*, New York, 1888

Rebecca Latimer Felton, *My Memoirs of Georgia Politics*, Atlanta, 1911

Thomas E. Watson, *Life and Speeches*, Thomson, 1911

Nathaniel E. Harris, *Autobiography*, Macon, 1925

Erskine Caldwell, *Tobacco Road* [1932], Savannah, 1974

Erskine Caldwell, *God's Little Acre*, New York, 1933

Erskine Caldwell, *The Journeyman*, New York, 1964

Erskine Caldwell, *Trouble in July*, New York, 1940

VI. SOCIAL PROBLEMS AND PROGRESS, 1908–63

1. Studies and Articles

L. Moody Simms, Jr., "A Note on Sidney Lanier's Attitude toward the Negro and toward Populism," *GHQ*, LII, 1968

A. Elizabeth Taylor, "The Origins and Development of the Convict Lease System in Georgia," *GHQ*, xxvi, 1942

Derrell Roberts, "Joseph E. Brown and the Convict Lease System," *GHQ*, XLIV, 1960

A. Elizabeth Taylor, "Abolition of the Convict Lease System in Georgia," *GHQ*, xxvi, 1942

W. E. B. DuBois, "The Negro Landholder of Georgia," *Bulletin of the Department of Labor*, Washington, 1901

Horace Calvin Wingo, "Race Relations in Georgia 1872–1908," unpublished Ph.D. dissertation, University of Georgia, 1969

R. B. Brooks, "A Local Study of the Race Problems," *Political Science Quarterly*, xxvi, 1911

John Hammond Moore, "Jim Crow in Georgia," *South Atlantic Quarterly*, LXVI, 1967

Clarence A. Bacote, "Negro Proscriptions, Protests and Proposed Solutions in Georgia, 1880–1908," *JSH*, XXV, 1959

C. Vann Woodward, "Tom Watson and the Negro in Agrarian Politics," *JSH*, IV, 1938

Robert M. Saunders, "The Transformation of Tom Watson," *GHQ*, LIV, 1970

Dewey W. Grantham, "Georgia Politics and the Disfranchisement of the Negro," *GHQ*, XXII, 1948

Dewey W. Grantham, *Hoke Smith and the Politics of the New South*, Baton Rouge, 1958

Louis T. Rigdon II, *Georgia's County Unit System*, Decatur, 1961

James C. Bonner, "Legislative Apportionment and County Unit Voting in Georgia since 1777," *GHQ*, XLVII, 1963

Ralph Wardlaw, *Negro Suffrage in Georgia, 1867–1930*, Athens, 1932

Frank Tannenbaum, *Darker Places of the South*, New York, 1924

I. A. Newby, *Jim Crow's Defense*, Baton Rouge, 1965

Charles S. Johnson, *The Negro in American Civilization*, New York, 1930

Charles S. Johnson, *Patterns of Negro Segregation*, New York, 1943

Gunnar Myrdal, *An American Dilemma*, New York, 1944

Charlton Moseley, "Latent Klanism in Georgia, 1890–1915," *GHQ*, LVI, 1972

Clement C. Moseley, "Invisible Empire: A History of the Ku Klux Klan in Twentieth Century Georgia, 1915–65," unpublished Ph.D. dissertation, University of Georgia, 1968

Charles O. Jackson, "William J. Simmons," *GHQ*, L, 1966

John Moffatt Mecklin, *The Ku Klux Klan*, New York, 1924

David M. Chalmers, *Hooded Americanism*, New York, 1965

Richard Sterner, *The Negro's Share*, New York, 1943

Arthur F. Raper, *The Tragedy of Lynching*, Chapel Hill, 1933

John Dollard, *Caste and Class in a Southern Town*, New York, 1937

Clement C. Moseley, "The Case of Leo Frank, 1913–15," *GHQ*, LI, 1967

Twelve Southerners, *I'll Take My Stand*, New York, 1930

Hal Steed, *Georgia, Unfinished State*, New York, 1942

Sue Bailes, "Eugene Talmadge and the Board of Regents Controversy," *GHQ*, LIII, 1969

Sarah McCulloh Lemmon, "The Ideology of Eugene Talmadge," *GHQ*, XXXVIII, 1954

William L. Belvin, Jr., "The Georgia Gubernatorial Primary of 1946," *GHQ*, L, 1966

R. Ray McCain, "Reactions to the U. S. Supreme Court Segregation Decision of 1954," *GHQ*, LII, 1968

Paul Douglas Bolster, "Civil Rights Movements in Twentieth Century Georgia," unpublished Ph.D. dissertation, University of Georgia, 1972

Sarah McCulloh Lemmon, *The Public Career of Eugene Talmadge, 1926–36*, Chapel Hill, 1952

Bruce Galphin, *The Riddle of Lester Maddox*, Atlanta, 1968

2. Printed Sources

Sir George Campbell, *White and Black*, London, 1879

Ray Stannard Baker, *Following the Color Line*, New York, 1908

Ralph McGill, *South and the Southerner*, Boston, 1959

Index